Praise for *Live Big*

"With Ajit Nawalkha's expert guidance, you'll tap into the magic ingredient that can help your organization sink or swim: your own outlook. Do not make the fatal flaw of thinking this sounds too simple to matter to you—it's absolutely crucial. Ajit's advising guidance has more than transformed my business; it's transformed my mind-set. I am forever grateful."

—Lisa Nichols, *New York Times* bestselling author and CEO of Motivating the Masses

"*Live Big* is a beautiful manifesto to entrepreneurs, change makers, and professionals. Beautifully written, a powerful wake-up call for anybody who wants to take their life to the next level."

—Vishen Lakhiani, founder and CEO of Mindvalley

"An unconventional approach for entrepreneurs to create a life on their terms. It's packed with insights, reframes, and perspectives. A fresh approach, Ajit trusts the entrepreneur to know the 'how-to' and 'tactical' stuff. *Live Big* focuses on the key to business success: the person actually running the business."

—Christine Hassler, master coach, international speaker, and bestselling author

"We secretly hope that success is a destination. And that one day, we'll finally arrive. But it doesn't seem to work that way. In fact, the more successful you become the greater the challenges you often face. Ajit is a secret guide to that paradox. He's an entrepreneur who has built multimillion-dollar businesses and helped others to do the same. But he does it from the inside out. You see, if strategy and tactics were all that worked, you'd just read Richard Branson's biography and become a billionaire. Instead, you need to go deeper—much deeper. If you want to *Live Big*, I highly recommend that you let Ajit be one of your guides."

—Rich Litvin, master coach and coauthor of *The Prosperous Coach*

"I have just started the book. I love it. I have this feeling that you are talking to me, but I would have never thought I was your audience. I feel excited and grateful . . . knowing that there is something that is just for me within these pages that I never thought to ask. I love the tone and am excited for the journey."

—Tiffany Persons, founder of Tiffany Casting Company and Shine on Sierra Leone

"Finally, a book that considers the entrepreneur and their personal emotional states. *Live Big* is a perspective and insightful guide, which in just few passages shifts the way you approach your business and life more powerfully."

—Rajesh Setty, cofounder of Audvisor and author of *Smart, but Stuck: When Being Brilliant is Not Good Enough*

LIVE BIG

THE ENTREPRENEUR'S GUIDE TO PASSION, PRACTICALITY, AND PURPOSE

AJIT NAWALKHA

BenBella Books, Inc.
Dallas, TX

BenBella Books, Inc.
10440 N. Central Expressway, Suite 800
Dallas, TX 75231
www.benbellabooks.com
Send feedback to feedback@benbellabooks.com

Printed in the United States of America
10 9 8 7 6 5 4 3 2 1

Library of Congress Cataloging-in-Publication Data
Names: Nawalkha, Ajit, author.
Title: Live big : the entrepreneur's guide to passion, practicality, and
  purpose / by Ajit Nawalkha.
Description: Dallas, TX : BenBella Books, Inc., [2018] | Includes
  bibliographical references and index.
Identifiers: LCCN 2018031878 (print) | LCCN 2018033927 (ebook) | ISBN
  9781946885678 (electronic) | ISBN 9781946885425 (paper over board : alk.
  paper)
Subjects: LCSH: Entrepreneurship. | Small business—Management. | Creative
  ability in business.
Classification: LCC HB615 (ebook) | LCC HB615 .N41999 2018 (print) | DDC
  658.4/09—dc23
LC record available at https://lccn.loc.gov/2018031878

Editing by Vy Tran
Copyediting by J. Patricia Connolly
Proofreading by Greg Teague and Cape Cod Compositors, Inc.
Text design by Publishers' Design and Production Services, Inc.
Text composition by PerfecType, Nashville, TN
Illustrations by Ng Siow Foon
Cover design by Sarah Avinger
Cover photo courtesy of Lost and Taken
Printed by Lake Book Manufacturing

Distributed to the trade by Two Rivers Distribution, an Ingram brand
www.tworiversdistribution.com

Special discounts for bulk sales (minimum of 25 copies) are available.
Please contact Aida Herrera at aida@benbellabooks.com.

To Neeta. You make *this* fun.

CONTENTS

PART 3: MAGIC

INTRODUCTION

Be fearless in the pursuit of what sets your soul on fire.

—Jennifer Lee

Why Live Big?
Because you must.

If you turn away from this calling, you'll struggle with a nagging, uncomfortable feeling that something's missing.

You'll experience a consistent sense of lack. You'll feel unfulfilled and unsatisfied.

In her bestselling memoir, *The Top Five Regrets of the Dying*, Bronnie Ware, an Australian nurse who worked in palliative care for many years, recorded the epiphanies her patients had as they faced the end of their lives. She found that one of the biggest regrets people most often expressed was, "I wish I'd had the courage to live a life true to myself, not the life others expected of me."

Most of us shy away from living the life we truly want to live.

Deep down, we all want to live big. You want to live big.

Here's the truth:

You were born to live your purpose.

You were born to serve at your highest potential.

You were born to become the best version of yourself.

You were born to be unapologetically you.

You were born to Live Big.

That's why I wrote this book.

I didn't always live big. I grew up in a house with twenty-two other people, in the ancient town of Jaipur, India. I was fortunate to have amazing parents. I was not as fortunate about having my own space. My brother and I shared a room. This room was also our study room, our bedroom, our playroom, and when guests stayed over, it was the guest room. My father was completely honest with me. He said, "I can help you get an education, son. I'll do everything I can to support your studies for as long as you need. But I don't have anything to offer you beyond that."

I will be forever grateful for his candor. I will forever appreciate that he loved me enough to be honest with me because it made me realize, early on in life, that if I wanted to live in a way that felt good in my soul, I'd have to make my own way. I instinctively knew there was more to life than just being someone who had a great education. I knew I was smart. I knew I was curious and interested about the world. I knew I wanted to Live Big.

I'll be straight with you—I didn't do well as a student. But I've done pretty well as a lifelong learner. Now, I feel compelled to share what I've discovered and experienced from the streets of Jaipur to high-powered boardrooms across the world. I want you to know that if I can create a life and business that fire me up every single day, you can too.

I've packed this book with the most important teachings and knowledge I've gained from some of the world's top business leaders, teachers, and coaches—many of whom I'm honored and grateful to call my friends.

This book also draws from my personal experiences. From childhood memories to my times working for a voluntary organization to my own early failures—and how I hustled through them. From my connections, interactions, and learnings as a master business coach and CEO of Mindvalley to the most important and game-changing insights I gained while cocreating a profoundly transformational company like Evercoach. You'll also discover ideas and lessons from my mentors who have built education-based businesses that are designed to bring about positive changes in the world.

As an entrepreneur, you need to know that your business isn't an entity. It's an *experience*. It's unfolding at every moment— when you work with a client, when you develop your marketing, when you lead your team. Every moment is vital. Critical.

And every moment is also an emotional roller coaster. You'll feel challenged. You'll wonder if it will all work out. You'll have doubts. Questions. You'll hear suggestions that push you to the limits of your belief system that are in direct opposition to popular consensus or to what most people would call "common sense."

The only way to handle the chaos and the crazy beauty of it all is this: know that growing your business is actually about growing yourself. It's about expanding into your potential. It's about how you manage your emotions, how you live your beliefs and values, how you expand your thinking. It's about staying sane, centered, and focused. The entrepreneur who does this will create a profitable enterprise that lasts.

Understand that new ideas and new technology are significant but they are not critical elements of success. Becoming a master at both life and entrepreneurship is about understanding yourself and your relationship with others. As we go through life, we go through multiple mental, spiritual, and emotional states. It's our ability to manage these states and to connect deeply and authentically with others that will make us successful, happy entrepreneurs.

I believe that each of us has the power to create meaningful lives and businesses but that this can happen only when we go deep and tap into that authentic, inspired, empowered space within. This conviction allowed me to rise from humble beginnings to do what I do today—work with incredible people from all walks of life, including legendary leaders and world changers. I do my part to build a world where everyone has the opportunity to live a fulfilling, joyful, abundant life. I still can't believe this is what I get to do all day, every day. It was just a distant dream for the longest time and now it's a reality.

I'm where I am today because I found that powerful place inside myself. It's a place that is in all of us, and I've written *Live Big* so you can find it too.

This is a concise, unique, edgy resource written for transformational leaders, rockstar entrepreneurs, and future innovators and igniters of positive change. This is not a guidebook. It's not a book on strategy. It might not be the book you want, but it is the book you need. You need it today. You will need it as your life unfolds and as your business expands.

Live Big is my invitation to you to walk the path toward greatness:

to rise up to the challenge

to build a truly amazing business

and to become the person you know you can be.

Let's bring you back home to your most powerful self.

HOW TO READ
THIS BOOK

Most authors expect you to read their books from cover to cover. There is a sequential story, process, and strategy. Something that takes you from point A to point B.

Live Big is not that kind of book.

Live Big is like life—there is no sequence. There is only flow. In life, one thing does not follow another in an orderly fashion. Things happen all at the same time. These events impact us in countless ways and create our deepest beliefs and values that in themselves can be disempowering.

Think of this book as your personal empowerment tool, your manual for greatness. Refer to it when you're facing a challenge. Read it when you need a bit of motivation. Dive into it when you're looking for inspiration. Pick it up when you are going through the chaos, the complexity, the confusion, and the incomparable, divine satisfaction of becoming the best version of yourself as you build a business that makes a difference in the world.

I'd love for you to trust your insight and think, "Show me what I need to read." Then open this book at random and absorb the message that you are meant to see. Believe me, you will read what you are supposed to read at the exact time you need to read it. With this book you don't need to follow a chapter-by-chapter order. You just need to follow your heart.

Having said all that, I know some of you love frameworks and guidelines, and, yes, sequence—and that's okay too. If this describes your approach, you'll be happy to know that this book is divided into three parts—*Meaning, Mojo,* and *Magic.*

Strategies alone don't create a meaningful life.

Methodologies alone don't create success.

Techniques alone don't create happiness and freedom.

It's *passion, purpose, and practicality* that will create a life and a business that matter.

The world's top entrepreneurs know that strategies, methodologies, and techniques are a fundamental part of building a great business. But more important, they understand that what matters more than all of this—the elements that will bring their desires and dreams to life—is their passion, their purpose, and the practical application of what they learn from their experiences as they grow and change.

In part 2, we're focusing on mojo, your unique essence, your inner power. You'll understand exactly what makes you tick—the things that move you and inspire you. You'll be clear about the beliefs that hold you back. You'll begin to understand what freedom truly means and how you can get it and use it to your advantage. You'll get to know yourself better than before, and, more important, you'll learn how to dissolve self-doubt so you can trust yourself to make the right decisions for your business.

Part 3 is about creating magic—exponential results—in your outer world. You'll discover game-changing, mind-shifting tactics and techniques that will elevate your relationship with other people. You'll learn to look at money and time—the elements that make up your external environment and are crucial to your success—in a whole new way. You'll discover how to work with smart, passionate people and how to give them room to grow. You'll learn that allowing them to be themselves will give you so much more in return. You'll reinvent your concept of time and reframe your ideas about money, and you'll learn to nurture and maximize your energy—the force within—to amplify your impact on the world.

Before you get started, here's something I'd love for you to do. Keep this book where you can get to it easily—on your desk or bedside table. Keep it visible so that when you need clarity and direction, you can pick it up and let it be your guiding light.

As you become who you are meant to be, as you build the business of your dreams, think of this book as your trusted friend—the one who isn't afraid to say the hard things. The friend that will give you the essential power to move forward, no matter what.

The one who leads you to new ideas so you can fly.

LIVE BIG Online Experience

This book comes with a Free Online Program to support your journey to living big! This means you'll have unlimited access to hours of additional in-depth, high-value training, practices, and content designed to help you fully absorb and implement the insights, techniques, systems, and ideas you've discovered in these pages. If you want to know more about a specific concept or find exercises that can help you embody some of the principles mentioned, you can find them on the website.

This unique online experience also includes awesome downloadable extras such as posters, photos, and videos—all easily available on the web and on Android and iOS.

When you dive into the Live Big Online Experience, you'll have access to:

- active, transformational training for entrepreneurs that's designed to create real-world results.
- additional strategies and proven techniques to rapidly uplevel all aspects of your business and life.
- tasks and exercises to skyrocket your personal and professional growth.
- a dynamic, interactive community of like-minded entrepreneurs who will share your journey and give you the support you need . . . and *so* much more!

Access Live Big Online Experience here: LiveBigTheBook.com/Tools.

PART ONE

Meaning

PASSION CONUNDRUM

YOU HAVE MANY
PASSIONS...

...START SOMEWHERE

CHAPTER 1

The Passion Conundrum

I would rather die of passion than of boredom.

—Vincent van Gogh

Follow your passion.

Do what feels good and you'll succeed.

Let your dreams be your guide and you'll find your purpose.

You've heard it all before and it feels like great advice. What's not to love? Living a life that reflects your passion and then turning that passion into profits—that's perfect, right?

Except that it's not. It's bad advice. At the very least, it's incomplete, especially for an entrepreneur. There are many reasons why and here's the biggest one: passions come and go; they never stay the same.

You travel to a new country and you're excited about the cuisine. You think to yourself, "I should open a restaurant that serves this food back home." You get home, do a little research, ask around, and realize there's a lot more to opening a restaurant than you thought. Suddenly, you're not excited about your restaurant idea anymore.

So, you let it go.

A couple of weeks later you happen to read an article about online selling. You get fired up again and you feel that adrenaline rush again. You tell your friends you're going to sell online in a big way. You start thinking about what you'd like to offer your soon-to-be customers. You might even make a list of ideas—but then, you can't make up your mind.

So, you let it go.

Now, you're at the point where you start to wonder, "What's going on?"

Here's the truth: passion is unpredictable. Passion is erratic, random, fickle.

You get caught up in it, in the moment, and it lights up your whole life. But often, over time, that fire fades. And then you get caught up in a new passion. Rinse and repeat. This isn't a bad thing if you know what's going on: your passion will not stand still. Your passion will grow and then diminish and grow again. Sometimes it will disappear. Feeling passionate about many different things, concepts, and ideas as you move through your life and business—that's not a curse; *it's a gift.* I learned this through personal experience.

I remember lying in bed staring at the ceiling for the fifth night in a row. I had just one thought and it repeated in my mind, over and over again. *Why the heck did I want to let go of the best thing that ever happened to me?* At the time, I was the CEO of a multimillion dollar company. It was a company driven by passion. It was rated as one of the best, most democratic places to work on the planet. I'd been dreaming about getting that job in that company for more than four years before I finally got my foot in the door. Now, I was heading the entire operation. I was at the top. This was supposed to be it. This was the thing that I would do for the rest of my life. It was what the boy from a gritty neighborhood in Jaipur, India, was meant to do with his life.

It made my parents proud. It made my friends proud. Heck, some of them even said I was *the* success story from our neighborhood. The one who'd "made it" out in the real world. This job was supposed to give me everything I wanted. It was supposed to be my deepest passion—except that it wasn't.

Despite being a hopelessly young, clueless soul at that time, I knew there was something else I needed to do. There was something I could sense in myself that was bigger than being CEO of an amazing company. This "something" felt fulfilling and faintly familiar. It hinted at who I could become. The passion that I once had to be part of this company—and by the way, I still think it's one of the best places to work in this world—had dramatically shifted. And that shift was incredibly annoying. I was about to piss away one of the best opportunities of my life and I knew there was no way around it.

Soon after I became CEO, I'd realized something that scared me. I'd found a new passion, and it was about contribution and innovation. This new passion started as a tiny flame that I'd managed to ignore, but it soon became a roaring fire. It drove me so far over the edge, I was starting to hurt the company I had sworn to protect and grow.

The force was strong. It overpowered me.

So, I quit the job. I let go of being CEO. I leaped into the unknown. This took some courage and it also took a certain

amount of stupidity. I was so naïve then. I didn't fully understand what I was doing, but in the years to come, I would discover the truth—and it was the truth about passion. The sooner
you know this truth, and the sooner you accept it, the easier it
will be for you to sail smoothly through life.

The thing is, passion is like your daily meal plan. In the
beginning, if you add all your favorite foods in the plan, you will
love your meal. But as you have the same meal for the fourth
day, the fifth day, and so on, you will start to get bored. The fact
is, your meal plan needs to evolve, and so does your passion.

A new spice, a new flavor is needed that will make your
meal a hearty one.

Understand this: the object of your passion will not stand
still. It will change. Heck, if it doesn't, you'll end up bored and
you don't want to be bored. You want to enjoy your life while
living your passion, don't you? Your passion is the voice of your
soul; it's in the way you express yourself. Embrace it in the light
of how it shows up at any given moment.

Follow your passion but don't allow it to imprison you with
fear. Don't get caught up in what your life will look like next
week or even tomorrow. Don't worry if your feelings about your
passion will change, because guess what? Those changes will
happen. I guarantee it. So, what should you do instead?

Play with your passion.

Allow it to shift, grow, and contract.

See how it feels when you mess around with it.

Ignore it and see if it stays.

If it does, give it some extra love and watch how it grows.

Chase your passion. Just don't tie yourself to it.

Also, know that you are allowed to have more than one passion at a time and not all passions are made equal. My passion for cooking allows me to be creative. It's my way of meditating. It has nothing to do with my business. I have no intention of starting the world's best restaurant, or any restaurant for that matter. But my passion for writing—now that's different. I love writing. It gives me purpose. It satisfies my soul. It inspires me to create practical applications around it.

Know that your passion will sometimes knock you out.

It might bring you to your knees.

You might share it with the world and then realize nobody gives a shit.

But do it anyway.

To dive deeper into this topic, download free tools and advanced strategies at www.LiveBigTheBook.com/Tools.

UTOPIAN

PURPOSE

CURIOUS

INSPIRE   CHALLENGING

LOVING   EXCITEMENT

HONEST   SELFLESS

UNIQUE

                    BEAUTIFUL

        TRUE

CHAPTER 2

The Utopian Purpose

When you dance, your purpose is not to get to a place on the floor. It's to enjoy every step along the way.

—Wayne Dyer

What's our purpose? Why are we here? These would be tough questions to answer if we were trying to find a purpose for all of humanity. For example, if we were trying to answer existential questions such as, "Why do humans exist?"

But on a smaller scale, on an individual level—for me, for you—finding our purpose isn't just possible, it's imperative.

Let's take a journey together.

I want you to imagine paradise. A utopia. A perfect place. You can have everything here. Go ahead and picture it in your mind and feel it in your heart. Don't be afraid to imagine the details. What would this place be like? Who are the people who live there? What are their values and beliefs? What are the choices they make?

How about you? What would you be like in your utopia? How would you like to show up there? Don't try to rationalize. Don't use your head but instead use your heart. Feel your way into your utopia; see it in your mind.

When you do, you'll start to realize how much you love this place and how much you love your life in this place. Your utopia probably has no racial bias and no sexism. Everyone in your utopia is equal, everyone is loved. You might find yourself living fully, fearlessly. You might find yourself loving bravely. You might find yourself creating value for others.

Got that picture in your mind? Feel that in your heart? Guess what? *That* right there—that's your purpose. Your purpose is to create that utopia, the world you want to live in. Your purpose is to live your way into the truest, most alive version of yourself.

Now that I've said that, how does that feel for you? Does the idea of having this purpose to create your utopia liberate you? Does it motivate you?

Or does it make you feel anxious?

If it makes you feel anxious, you probably created your utopia from your head and not your heart. You created what you *think* is right. *What is the right thing to say? What would people think about my purpose?*

What will people think if I quit my high-profile job to write poetry?

What will my college friends think if I choose coaching executives over working on Wall Street?

What will my parents think if I don't join our family business but vlog my travels instead?

What will my partner think if I teach meditation to con-struction workers instead of working my soul-crushing job as an architect?

That's the kind of thinking that will kill your purpose.

My mother's favorite line is, *"Log kya kahenge,"* which is Hindi for, "What will people think?" But you are not here in this world to design your life according to random thoughts and opinions of others. Your life is yours and this means it's about how *you* think and how *you* feel.

Here's the thing about purpose no one talks about:

You don't have to go big with it. You don't have to impress anyone with it. Your purpose doesn't have to be about saving the world or changing lives.

It's *your* purpose. You get to choose.

Your purpose. Your choice.

I once worked with a client at a one-day intensive coaching course. She's in the photography business. Part of the intensive was about getting clear about her purpose. When it came time to share, I asked, "What's your purpose? Why do you do what you do?" Her answer: *my purpose is to create positive transfor-mations in the world.*

I'll admit, when I first heard that, it sounded great. It was clear that this client was operating from the heart. She cared about her customers and wanted to make a difference with her work, but something didn't feel right to me. We went a little deeper and it soon became clear. Her true purpose? *To help her customers use a camera to capture beautiful moments in their lives.*

That was it. And that was enough.

When you start thinking about your purpose in this life, it's tempting to come up with something epic. World-changing. All-encompassing.

You don't have to end world hunger. Or cure cancer. Or save endangered animals.

Your true purpose can be simple.

It could be about taking great pictures. It could be about living a life that is your own idea of freedom. It could be about enjoying all the luxury the world has to offer. It could be about living in a house by the beach and spending the rest of your days there with the one you love.

I have no grand purpose. My purpose is to Live Big, and to me, that means living as my true self, living with joy, creativity, inspiration, and contributing to a positive society. I want to love fully and serve passionately. I don't see problems in the world. I see only opportunities. Transformations. I don't see a world that needs fixing. I see a world that needs us living as our true selves.

We arrive on this planet as a blank canvas. Our true self at birth is beautiful, curious, selfless, loving. If we can just keep those qualities throughout our lives, we can indeed Live Big.

There's no grander purpose than that.

Purpose isn't about how big you go; it's about how real it feels. It's about being aligned. It's about what's true for you. And always know that it's not your job to save us all. Please, don't try to save us all.

Don't suck the joy out of living your purpose. If saving the world gives joy to you, go for it. More power to you. But don't do it just for us. First, do it for yourself.

Aspire to a purpose that is exciting. A little challenging. Very inspiring. You need something that makes you smile when you think about it, that lights you up. Know that you may never get to your purpose and know that getting to your purpose is never the point. Going for your purpose, pursuing your calling, showing up every day as the honest, true, full version of yourself. That's what we are aiming for.

More of that, and you're golden.

So, the only questions you need to ask when it comes to identifying your purpose are "What's true for me? What's the thing that's going to get me to leap out of bed every morning?" If you don't know the answer right now, that's okay.

Give yourself the space to find your purpose:

Live your purpose.

Create a meaningful life.

Take time to find what living big means to you. Whatever that is, it is perfectly perfect (except if it is illegal, or creates a mess for everyone else—then check if it's truly you because you probably just made up that shit).

I hope you can find your purpose. I know you will find your purpose—that beautiful, powerful light in you.

Your uniqueness. Your truth. That's what we need. And that's enough.

To dive deeper into this topic, download free tools and advanced strategies at www.LiveBigTheBook.com/Tools.

MATRIX OF PRACTI-CALITY

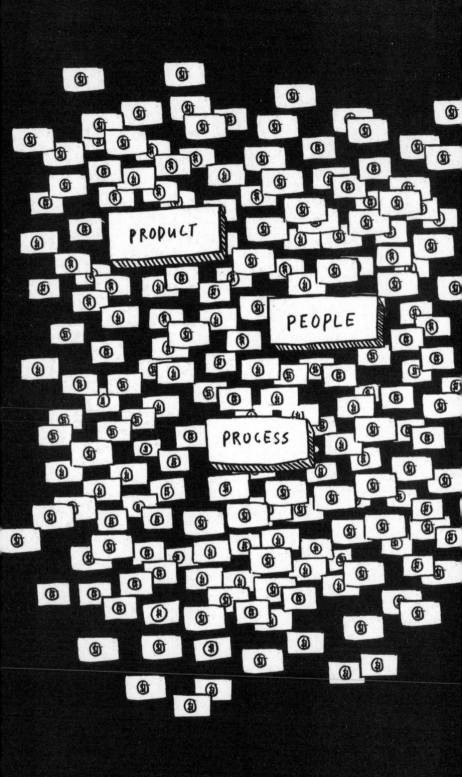

CHAPTER 3

The Matrix of Practicality

If you can't describe what you are doing as a process, you don't know what you're doing.

—W. Edwards Deming

Passion is your fuel.

Purpose is your destination.

Practicality is the map of the road.

When most entrepreneurs talk about their business, practicality rarely enters the conversation. This is a problem and it's a big one. Passion and purpose are important but practicality is the element that creates profits and prosperity.

Practicality allows you to support people.

Practicality builds systems and processes.

Practicality organizes and sparks growth.

When you create practicality in your business and when you adopt a practical mind-set, you'll clearly see the actions you need to take to hit your goals. Without practicality, no amount of passion is enough to carry you through to success as an entrepreneur. Without practicality, your purpose will remain out of reach because you will be unable to create what you are meant to create.

In an ideal world, all entrepreneurs would value practicality as much as passion and purpose, but that's not how it often goes down. Most businesses start with a ton of passion and purpose. It's pure grit. Hustle. Drive. Intention. Personal power. It's the nitro boost you see in those *Fast and Furious* movies. It gives you a big push. That big thrust that you need to get started.

Then it starts to wear off and there's nothing to fall back on.

When there is no practicality, you have nowhere to go but down. Your business will start to feel like a drag. You'll feel like you're doing the same thing again and again and again, and it's going to take a toll. You'll start to lose your steam. You'll start to wonder, "Why am I doing this? Why am I running this business?"

And you give up. Or you keep shifting your business's focus and in the process you lose time, money, and motivation.

I don't want you to end up like this.

I want you to think of your business as a whole new being. Just to be clear, I'm not suggesting that you think of your business as your baby. Some entrepreneurial and success books suggest this. I think it's total BS. Thinking of your business as your baby will ultimately destroy you. There's way too much attachment involved. Your business is *not* your baby. It's your masterpiece. Your creation. And like many other great creations in the world, it outlives the creator.

In this context, think of a van Gogh painting, Jay Z's music, or Walt Disney's empire.

If you're ready to create your own masterpiece—and I know you are because you're reading this book—then you need to introduce practicality in your business. You need a pragmatic approach. You need to find a way to bring your ideas and your inspiration into the real world. You need systems and processes so your business can keep running with or without you.

Getting practical about your business involves three things: product, people, and processes. I call it the Matrix of Practicality:

1. People want your product. There is a need for your product in the market.
2. You can find and keep people that will serve your business best.
3. You can build processes and scale your business.

If you have all three, then there is practicality at play, which means that not only do you get to live with passion and purpose but you get to have a business that actually makes money and supports you and your family.

First, let's talk about product.

One of the keys to finding practicality in business is to find a unique market, or submarket, that has a strong need or want. If you don't have ideas for a practical product, look at the market you want to play in. Your market space can give you these ideas if you dig deep.

Here's a great example. When Dollar Shave Club came to the market with their razors, many people thought their subscription box model was a silly concept. As their name suggests,

Dollar Shave Club offered low-cost monthly plans for razors, blades, and related grooming products like shave butter, moisturizers, and beard oils. They were going into competition with the likes of Gillette, which had advanced technology and was investing millions in creating a better razor. Moreover, Gillette for one was investing millions in marketing.

But Dollar Shave Club saw an audience no one was talking to. It was a market where the competitors and the big players didn't matter. It was a market where men just wanted a good shave. They didn't care about the technology; they cared for a cheap, quick, effective shave.

Dollar Shave Club created something practical the market wanted and it found enormous success. Eventually Dollar Shave Club was acquired by Gillette for a billion dollars. See how that works? A good product doesn't need to be complex. It just needs to be right for the market.

The second element in the matrix is people.

If we can't build a team around the business, it becomes an impractical business. The quality of your team will define the quality of your culture. It will define the quality of your clients and the quality of your output.

When Mindvalley, a global education tech startup focused on personal excellence and entrepreneurship, moved its base from New York City to Kuala Lumpur, Malaysia, we ran into a problem. Malaysia was still developing its talent pool. Certain skill sets, like copywriting, digital advertising, and launch managing, were either not easy to find or not available in the market. So we looked outside. It was easier to find these talents internationally. We were determined to find as many talented people as possible, so we spread the net wide. This translated into finding ways to attract talent from around the world. It was a smart, practical move. Today, the Mindvalley team consists of an amazing group of people from more than forty countries. A desire to find only the best talent gave us an opportunity to create a workplace with diverse cultures, and in the process it gave us perspectives from around the world, and allowed us international expansion. As a result, Mindvalley, one of the fastest growing companies in the area of personal excellence, is able to create a global school that delivers transformational education for people of all ages, ethnicities, and cultures.

Let's look at the final element in the matrix of practicality—processes.

Introducing processes is one of the greatest challenges you'll face in your business. You see, the way we've always done things is the way we always want to do things. We get really attached to the way something is done, and almost every entrepreneur I've ever met wants to do everything themselves. This is understandable, but it's an attitude and an approach that will limit your ability to expand your business and ultimately, it may even have a destructive effect.

This is why you must embrace processes. As hard or as complex as they may seem, processes are nothing more than a set flow of activities that help you and your team complete tasks in an effective way. New processes seem complicated because we're not familiar with them yet or we haven't found a way to motivate our teams to implement them. It's not because new processes are inherently complex.

When I work with my clients, I've noticed that the quicker they are able to let go of doing all the tasks themselves—the quicker they get comfortable with the question, *How can I never do this task again?*—the quicker they start building systems and processes that lead to a successful, profitable business that continues to grow and expand.

Let me give you an example. It was the final hours of our intensive session. We had invested the whole day in creating strategies around client acquisition. We had three clear strategies that we found would create a significant increase in revenue. It had been a productive day. Until my client—let's call him Jim—said, "This is amazing. Love it. Now I have to figure out how to make it happen."

An innocent statement that led to finding a deeper challenge with the company. You see, Jim had a bigger problem at hand than just client acquisition. He was the be-all and end-all of the business. He was needed by everyone on staff. He was doing most tasks himself. Jim was great at doing things, but his overinvolvement in tasks that could be left to his team had become the reason for stagnating growth.

So we invested the rest of the day in finding out what Jim did and the sequence of activities he would perform to get there. Then we created a flowchart of activities he could have his team deliver instead. As these processes got deployed to the team, Jim started to have more time on his hands. Jim could then start working *on* the business, not *in* it. As he found more time in his day, he could focus on growth strategies, creative ideas, and strategic partnerships instead of managing the day-to-day tasks.

Think about it: If we never move from a place of doing the same thing again and again, if we never let go of doing everything ourselves, if we never implement practical processes, how will we get to a place where we can fully serve our purpose and fully live our passion?

Remember this: passion is not commitment. Purpose is not commitment. But introduce practicality and that's when the magic happens. You'll have the commitment you need to push through all the obstacles and challenges in your journey. Practicality is where you lay out a product, build a team, and lay systems so this product makes it to the market and you can build a business around it. Introducing practicality in business begs for commitment.

That's the space where passion, purpose, and practicality intersect.

That's the space where you get to serve and love at your highest level.

That's the space where profits start to flow.

That's the space where you get to live your dreams.

To dive deeper into this topic, download free tools and advanced strategies at www.LiveBigTheBook.com/Tools.

PART 2

Mojo

HAPPY FIRST

FOLLOW YOUR HEART.

BUT FIRST,

KNOW YOUR HEART.

CHAPTER 4

Happy First

Let your joy be in your journey—not in some distant goal.

—Tim Cook

I f you look closely, you'll see that many of the legendary entrepreneurial stories that inspired you to start your business are actually sad. Some of these stories are even quite depressing.

There's the eccentric billionaire who can't stay in a relationship and always ends up alone. There's the genius who's also an asshole that everyone secretly hates. There's the celebrity who's also a sex addict. And let's not forget all those "successful" entrepreneurs who give up their happiness and health to get to the top.

The message we receive is clear—great success can only be achieved with great sacrifice.

You must put *everything* on the line to get what you want, right?

Wrong.

Incomplete.

Overly dramatic.

Most important—disempowering.

If you think you must sacrifice everything, if you are looking to let go of all the joy from your life just because you want to do something amazing for the world, I'm appealing to you now: please don't put that pressure on the rest of us.

Heck, don't put that pressure on yourself.

Yes, we need people who want to change the world, but we don't need the burden of your destroyed life to get there. What the world needs is your positive energy and a great example of success for the next generation. What the world needs is more joy and fulfillment for you and for all of us. You see, building something incredible, creating something special, and bringing your genius out into the world doesn't have to rise from the grave of your soul, your health, your joy, and your relationships.

It must be *fueled* by your soul, your health, your joy, and your relationships.

We could all use a healthy, happy Steve Jobs. We need him to be here with us, helping to create a brilliant future, and better technologies for decades. But he was a genius who stressed his team to the max, pushed himself way beyond the line, and left us too soon.

The legend isn't enough. The story isn't enough.

Yes, we should have the drive to create the impossible and we should make the impossible possible. We just don't need to die doing it. That same Steve, whose life story is unfortunately an excuse for many CEOs to act like assholes, said this in his famous commencement speech at Stanford:

Remembering that I'll be dead soon is the most important tool I've ever encountered to help me make the big choices in life because almost everything—all external expectations, all pride, all fear of embarrassment or failure—these things just fall away in the face of death, leaving only what is truly important. Remembering that you are going to die is the best way I know to avoid the trap of thinking you have something to lose. You are already naked. There is no reason not to follow your heart.

Follow your heart. *Follow your heart.*
But before you follow, *know your heart.*
Our hearts seek love, play, and peace. Our hearts want to be happy. Our hearts long for joy.
You want to be happy. You want joy.
You are a loving, kind soul who desires to be good to others and to yourself. Connect with that goodness within you and put your happiness first. Do it because you are going to die. That sounds morbid, I know, but it's also true.
All you have is this moment, this experience. Make it an interesting one. Make it fun. Make it worth sharing.
You don't have to be a sad success story. You can be an inspiring, happy one.

To dive deeper into this topic, download free tools and advanced strategies at www.LiveBigTheBook.com/Tools.

THIS IS

HOW YOU

DIE

CHAPTER 5

This Is How You Die

Doubt is a pain too lonely to know that faith is his twin brother.

—Khalil Gibran

W. Timothy Galleway was a nationally ranked tennis player as a boy. While on sabbatical from an office administration job at Harvard, he started work as a tennis instructor. At the start, he stuck to traditional methods of instruction—the technique, the swing. His students were getting results, but improvements were slow and inconsistent.

Galleway grew curious. He soon discovered that if he simply got his students to focus on their strokes, technique evolved naturally and seemed to self-correct. Players using Gallewey's new methods improved far more rapidly than usual, and it happened without self-criticism or trying hard to do it the "right" way.

You see, most of us understand what's right for us when it comes to starting and running a successful business. But then we start looking for confirmation. We adopt a different approach because someone—usually someone who seems to be more successful—tells us what to do and how to do it. This compels us to try and "get it right." So, we look outside ourselves for validation. We go against our instincts.

When this happens, doubt creeps in. Doubt about abilities and skills. Doubt about what we should do. Doubt about the outcome.

Doubt is where your business goes to die.

In fact, this book nearly died before it was written because I let doubt get in the way.

Before Microsoft, Bill Gates cocreated a business around processing raw data for engineers. That business failed.

Father of the automobile, Henry Ford, created a company before he started the Ford Motor Company. It was called the Detroit Automobile Company. It went bankrupt.

Colonel Sanders pitched his Kentucky Fried Chicken recipe to 1,009 people before someone said they'd try it.

Every one of these legends is human, which means every one of them felt doubt cast its dark shadow over them. Imagine if they'd stopped at the first sign of failure. Imagine if they'd listened to everyone else. Imagine if they'd let doubt kill their dreams. No. They fought back and found their power. They created magic. They changed the world on their terms.

You have a natural ability to think—grow, progress, create, analyze, recalibrate. But doubt disrupts all of this. It blocks out possibilities and creates internal interference. When you quiet this interference, you can tap into your natural abilities with greater ease.

About four years ago, I was doing deep work exploring who I was and what I wanted, both for the world and for myself. As I questioned everything and evaluated everything I thought I knew, I felt a need to speak, share my message, and create transformations for people around the world. I felt an inner drive—a calling—that was so powerful I couldn't ignore it. I knew I had something great to offer and I knew I could do it while having fun. I could contribute and grow at the same time and nothing excited me more than this realization.

Here's something you should know about me. I like to allow new ideas and thoughts to marinate for a bit so they can get some flavor going in there. I like my ideas to get juicy before I slice a small part of it and present it to my small, trusted group of advisors, mentors, and friends. So, when I first got the idea to become a speaker, I played around with it in my mind. I leaned into it and gave it thought and attention. Then I shared it with my group.

Well, I wasn't ready for what happened next.

One of these advisors came back to me and said, "No one wants to listen to an Indian guy with a thick accent on stage." Ouch! I know this man really, *really* well. I know he had good intentions and that he wanted only the best for me, but that comment burned. I felt the heat of it all the way through my heart.

And it opened the door for doubt to walk right in.

Doubt instantly started to do its thing with my mind and it made me want to quit the idea of speaking even before I landed my first gig. Soon after that first blow, things got even worse. My doubt doubled in strength when a colleague made a passing comment, "If you are not a white female, you have no chance at making it big in coaching and speaking."

Double ouch! These are some of the most inspiring, confident individuals telling me, "Who are you kidding? It's not going to work for you, buddy."

Ever have that happen to you?

It took me another twelve months to find the courage to step on that stage and let faith win over doubt. I had to find the belief that my accent wouldn't matter. Neither would my looks. Being brown doesn't mean I can't facilitate change. It's only a problem if you are racist!

In the end, I did get to do what I thought I could do. What I wanted to do.

And now, you are reading this book because I crushed that doubt. While I write this, I am still brown, I'm a guy, and yes, I still have my Indian accent.

So, to hell with them all. To hell with not believing in yourself.

Crush doubt. Kill it. It's the best thing you can ever do for yourself.

It's the best thing you can do for the world.

To dive deeper into this topic, download free tools and advanced strategies at www.LiveBigTheBook.com/Tools.

KNOW
THYSELF

CHAPTER 6

Know Thyself

He who knows others is wise. He who knows himself is enlightened.

—Lao Tzu

K now thyself. It's a maxim that's been passed down through the centuries. The origin remains unclear, but it was used in the teachings of the Greek philosopher, Socrates, and then it was captured in the writings of his celebrated student, Plato.

It's a saying that carries a depth of wisdom that may be hard to grasp at first, but it's worth the effort because there is no real happiness or fulfillment when there is no knowledge and understanding of self.

(Phew, that was deep, huh?!)

Now, let's break it down:

When you know yourself, you can get to your personal truth. You'll know your motivations, aspirations, and inspirations. You'll be intimately connected to your beliefs, your values, and your principles. When you understand your inner world in this way, you'll come to know not just *what* you want and *how* to acquire what you want. You'll finally discover *why* you want what you want.

And this is where things start to get interesting. Knowing *why* you want what you want will shift the entire game. It will change your perspective about life because why you want what you want is ultimately about *how you want to feel.*

Think about your life and think about where you are now. Get really quiet and be honest with yourself.

At that point, you will come to see that there are three key emotions that you're looking for: love, joy, and appreciation.

If you think back, you'll realize you've been searching for these feelings all your life. It's why you chose to do what you do. It's the reason you became who you are. You want to serve because you want to feel these feelings. You've been drawn to *give* love, joy, and appreciation to others because you want the same for yourself.

Take a moment to take that in. *(No, really, take a moment. It's okay.)*

You might feel like I'm suggesting you're selfish. It might feel like I'm saying you're doing all that you do, that you want to be of service, because you want something for yourself.

Let me tell you this: you're *not* wrong.

You *are* doing what you do because you want something—you need something—for yourself. You cannot give something to others when you are empty inside. There is no shame in wanting to be recognized and wanting to feel loved and appreciated. There is no guilt in wanting joy in your life.

We live in a world of exchange and of balance. Yin and yang are always at play.

Where there is darkness there is light.

Where there is joy, there is sorrow.

You give and you receive.

You fall and you rise.

You live and you die. (*And according to some belief systems, you live again!*)

This is the way of nature. This is the balance of life.

So, admit and embrace the truth. Seek to know yourself. Accept yourself.

You want to feel a certain way. Know that this is okay. This is more than okay; it's awesome. Wanting love, joy, and appreciation is a beautiful thing. You need it almost as much as the air you breathe.

Why?

Because when you feel this way, you are rejuvenated and replenished from within. You'll serve others from your highest level. You'll serve from the heart and you'll reach and exceed even your own expectations.

But this is just the first step to knowing yourself.

Now that you know how you want to feel, let me ask you this—*how do you get there?*

How can you start to feel that love, joy, and appreciation you've been searching for pretty much all your life? The good news is that you're already on the path. It's something you may not realize at the moment.

I have an important truth for you.

Every time you set a goal in your business and in your work, and every time you hit that goal, you feel immersed in so much love and joy. You feel appreciated and grateful for where you are and the work that you do.

But then it's over.

Sometimes it takes a minute or two, sometimes it takes a few weeks or months, but no matter how big your achievement, no matter how many goals you hit, you slide right back to the beginning.

Your feelings return to neutral.

This phenomenon is captured in what I call the Law of Infinite Growth, which states, "There is no destination. The closer you feel you are to your destination, that destination will only move further away. That's the challenge and beauty of life: the Journey itself."

That's why all of the good feelings you have when you arrive at your goal—your destination—disappear. It's because there *is* no destination.

That's why you always end up setting another, even bigger goal just so you can have another fleeting taste of these feelings again.

Some people never discover this truth. They go through their entire lives setting one goal after another. Each goal is bigger and more complicated than the last. They spend all of their time and energy in this life, hitting goals. Each time, they hope the next destination will finally and permanently give them the love and the joy and appreciation they crave.

But they never get there.

I was one of those people until I discovered a better way. It dawned on me that the chase for joy is futile. Joy and love are there for us at all times. They are not for us to earn or to seek and find.

When we have love and joy, when we show up with love and joy, appreciation will be waiting right there. Appreciation is given to us when we live authentically and in line with our values.

Most people don't see this. They believe goals and wins and achievements will give them what they seek. Our goals are there to give us satisfaction and fulfillment. Our goals will give us focus and direction. Our goals will allow us to be of service at greater and higher levels.

But our goals will *not* make us happy. Because there is never joy and love and appreciation and there is always joy and love and appreciation.

It all depends on you and your perspective.

Stop looking for these emotions outside yourself and learn to connect into your heart. Ask yourself, "What makes me feel loved and joyful and appreciated right now? In this moment?" Success will find you if you live this way and you stay true to what makes you happy and fulfilled, what makes you feel good about you. Joy will find you. Love will find you. Appreciation will be given to you, freely.

I'll share my personal tip for feeling good right in this moment. One of the greatest ways you can feel good in the now is to compare your current life to your past life. Do that instead of looking at your current life and comparing it against the goal that's ahead of you. When you look at your past life, you'll see just how far you've come and how much you've overcome. This will give you the motivation, the energy, and the personal power to move forward and do great things in this world.

The best part? You'll feel that joy, love, and a sense of appreciation even if you never achieve some of your goals.

There is immense power and freedom in this approach.

You won't need external accomplishments and validation. You'll be able to give that to yourself.

It will uplevel your ability to give freely to others with no expectations.

It will allow you to operate from a space of abundance instead of scarcity.

It will allow you to serve in a way that will create transformations for far more people than ever before—thousands more, maybe even millions more.

It will change your ability to create money and freedom and happiness.

And it all begins with two words:

Know thyself.

To dive deeper into this topic, download free tools and advanced strategies at www.LiveBigTheBook.com/Tools.

FLOW, YOU MUST

CHAPTER 7

Flow, You Must

May what I do flow from me like a river, no forcing and no holding back, the way it is with children.

—Rainer Maria Rilke

Flow is a mental, emotional, and spiritual state.

Flow is a state where you enter perfect immersion fueled by energized focus, and you experience a feeling of deep enjoyment as you move through an activity. This is the kind of state that will have you creating your best work. Your greatest masterpieces will come from this.

When you're in flow, building your business and striking off all those tasks from your to-do list will start to feel really good. You'll move efficiently, effectively, effortlessly from one moment to another.

Flow is a state of near supernatural focus and clarity, and as you can imagine, everyone wants to achieve it. Heck, I've wanted to *live* in flow from the day I first heard about it. I was introduced to the concept a few years ago when I watched a wildly popular TED Talk called "Flow, the Secret to Happiness." The talk was presented by Mihaly Csikszentmihalyi, a Hungarian-American psychologist and professor who first identified and named this state.

I was recently reading Steven Kotler's book *The Rise of Superman*, and a quote jumped out at me. It instantly made me think of the limitations on our potential when we're not operating in a state of flow:

> Most people live in a very restricted circle of their potential being. They make use of a very small portion of their possible consciousness, and of their soul's resources in general, much like a man who, out of his whole organism, should get into a habit of using and moving only his little finger.

Moving only his little finger . . .

Can you imagine the tragedy of this? You have a body and a brain that will allow you to do incredible, even impossible things, but you move just one finger. As an entrepreneur, achieving anything less than your highest potential is a major problem. The whole point of running your business—or at least a key part of it—is to get to a place where you can do what you are meant to do in this life. This is the place where you are at your best and serving at the highest level. You can only achieve this when you understand how to get yourself into a state of flow and stay there.

So, let's dive deeper into what flow is and isn't. Remember back when you used to prep for tests and exams in high school? How did you feel when you were facing an exam on a

subject you couldn't stand? You know what I'm talking about—
it's one of those subjects that made you feel kind of stupid. No
matter how hard you tried to concentrate, you just couldn't do
it. You just didn't get it. So, you ignored this subject all year
and then two days before the exam, you sat down and tried
to cram for it.

Then there are the subjects that felt like a waste of time. For
me, this was definitely English. I couldn't understand why I had
to study grammar and spell an endless list of words. What was
this, 1920s England? It would have been less boring to watch
paint dry. In my school kid's brain, it just didn't make sense. No
one I knew spoke mistake-free, grammatically correct English,
or had mastered the art of spelling every word perfectly, and
they all seemed to be doing fine!

I'm sure it will come as no surprise to you when I say I
scored shit in English in school, but here I am, writing this
book you're reading right now. My friend Lisa Nichols is a world
renowned, in-demand motivational speaker and author. She
often tells the story of how she was always a C-student in high
school. How her teachers told her she would never become a
writer. Now, she's a *New York Times* bestselling author.

My point is, not being able to do well in certain subjects
in school usually has very little to do with your intelligence or
your abilities. You didn't do well because you were mostly bored
out of your mind—no flow.

But everything changed when you were interested and
excited about what you were learning. I loved learning about
computer programming, math, and history in high school.
When it was time for exams, the "shit at English" loser became
a brilliant A-student in other subjects.

This isn't because I suddenly and inexplicably became ultra-smart. It was because I was curious and passionate about these subjects. I know you can recall subjects that brought out the genius in you in high school. How did you feel about them? Excited and engaged, right? Your teachers made it all feel fun and doable. You couldn't wait to dive in and learn more.

That's my personal secret to getting into flow. Get curious and excited about building your business. Get curious and excited about the tasks and the activities. Get curious and excited about sales, marketing, and everything else.

And here's a little more for you to chew on when you want to get into flow:

Research done by smart people like Kotler and, of course, the Father of Flow, Csikszentmihalyi, reveals that being in flow is directly influenced by two elements:

1. The quality of skill you possess
2. The level of the challenge

The balance between these two elements has to be *just* right.

As you progress and become a more seasoned entrepreneur, you will naturally acquire more and more business, technical, management, and personal skills. You will naturally improve at everything you do in your business. As you become better and better, tasks and activities that felt like major challenges or problems start to feel easier. Eventually, you reach a state where you are barely conscious of your skill in that area.

Let's take typing as another example. When you first learn how to use a keyboard, it feels like you're trying to grow wings to fly to the moon. It's awkward, uncomfortable, and just plain hard. You have to keep looking at the keys and even when you're slow and careful, you make mistakes in your typing. But if you stick to it, you'll get to a place where you don't even have to glance at the keyboard. Your speed improves. Your skill increases. Your confidence soars. It starts to feel effortless and you don't even have to think about it.

This is when you can get into flow *but* it's not how you stay there.

This is the tricky part. This is why our smart researchers highlight the second element—the level of the challenge. If you don't up the challenge, you'll find the work that was first hard and that you eventually got good at, the work that inspired your curiosity and excitement, will start to bore the crap out of you. Your enjoyment drops. Drastically. You start to *not* give a damn.

It all turns into those English exams I hated so much.

To avoid falling into a pit of boredom, you must increase the challenge and then that excitement and curiosity will return. The aim is to get to a place where you know you can do something but it's not easy. Those computer exams I loved to take? I knew how to code, but I didn't know which program would be featured in the test. When I got the questions, I didn't know the answers right away, but I knew I'd get to the answer. I knew I had the skill to take me there.

This is the beautiful place—the place of flow.

In business and in life, to create flow we need to stay curious and excited. We also need to consistently hone our skills and up the challenge. The more you are in flow, the more you can achieve.

The more you achieve, the closer you get to hitting your highest potential, and the more you can expand and improve your own life and the lives of others.

And that's what being an entrepreneur is all about.

To dive deeper into this topic, download free tools and advanced strategies at www.LiveBigTheBook.com/Tools.

THIS IS
FREEDOM

CHAPTER 8

This Is Freedom

None are more hopelessly enslaved than those who falsely believe they are free.

—Johann Wolfgang von Goethe

Imagine the day when it all finally falls into place. You wake up and you have everything you've ever wanted. That's not all. You realize that your desires have become your reality in exactly the way you wanted it to happen. You now have fame, fortune, glory, happiness, satisfaction, and freedom. More freedom than you've ever had in your life

Now you can do what you want to do. All day. Every day.

You might be going, "He's about to tell me that I can have it all if I just follow my dreams and blah, blah, blah." If this is what you're thinking, I don't blame you. So many coaches, courses, and books on personal development and entrepreneurship present you with a platter of clichés like "dreams do come true," and "just believe and you can make it happen" and all that stuff.

This is not that kind of book and I'm not that kind of coach.

I'm not going to tell you what you *want* to hear. I'm going tell you what you *need* to hear. Even if it's not pretty. Even if it

most of us start a business to find freedom
us find ourselves trapped in a prison of mis-
umptions about freedom.

I meet countless brilliant, new entrepreneurs all the time and when I ask them what they want, so many of them say to me, "I want to just lie on the beach and do nothing." My answer is always the same: "So go and do that." They're always startled when I say this. They expect me to tell them the only way to success is to hustle all day, every day.

But that's not what I tell them because I know something they don't (at least not at first) and it's this: lying on the beach and doing nothing is fantastic for a couple of days, a week, or maybe a month. But if you happen to have even a whisper of the entrepreneurial spirit in you, you can't lie on the beach for much longer than that. It would drive you crazy because the truth is that doing nothing on a beach for the rest of your life is not freedom.

It's laziness. It's killing yourself with boredom.

Freedom—true freedom—is choice. It's getting to choose whether you want to do something or not to do it. That is true freedom.

Freedom is a decision and a mind-set.

Freedom is also structure.

Here's the thing: you can have it all. You can have all the money, fame, happiness, and freedom you want, but to get there you need routine. Sequence. Specificity. Systems.

Structure.

No matter what you do, if you want to do it well, if you want to succeed, there is a structure that needs to be in place. There are pillars needed to support your progress. You must have a map that highlights the terrain.

When I tell people freedom is structure, I get a lot of push-back on that definition. When I say this on stage or when I'm speaking to clients, the complaints start:

"I hate structure."

"Structure kills creativity."

"Structure? That's like having a 9 to 5 job!"

Some of these complaints get a little personal. "You don't know what you're saying, Ajit. More structure? You've got to be kidding!"

I usually wait patiently for people to calm down and then I explain: you don't hate structure. You hate *other people's* structures. You hate structures someone else put in place.

Still not convinced? Still think you hate structure? Still feeling like structure is something you will never bow to?

Okay, let me ask you this:

Do you like your food served at a preferred temperature?

Do you like your clothes folded the way you like them?

Do you like hanging out with friends at a favorite bar?

Do you have a preferred brand of toothpaste?

Do you have a favorite movie you watch again and again?

Do you have a playlist you like to listen to when you work?

You like structure.

You like structure when you create it for yourself.

You would hate the world if there was no structure. If things just happened with no order, that would be complete chaos. It might be cool for a day or two, but you definitely don't want your entire life to be unstructured.

How do artists work? I was listening to an audiobook called *If You Want to Write* by Brenda Ueland, and there is a section in the book where she talks about the creative process of writing fiction. She says the process sometimes means just sitting with an idea for hours and hours. Sometimes it's sitting in front of your typewriter *(I guess Brenda's old school)* for hours until the words come to you.

You might think, "See, there is no structure to art. It's just waiting for the words to come."

Actually, there is a structure—it's just not what you would expect it to be. Sitting with a piece of paper, sitting with an idea is part of the structure of creating masterful writing. Going out and experiencing life is part of the structure of creating beautiful art. Skip the structure and art loses its essence. It loses its soul.

That's the way we need to think about freedom.

Freedom is like art. Sit with it. Reflect on it. See what comes up for you. Paint it in the way you feel it. Throw it away. Let it unfold again. Keep doing it until an idea arises—an idea that feels right.

When you hit on that gorgeous idea, that powerful juicy idea, take action.

Take that powerful idea, insight, image, or intuitive hit, take it and bring it into reality. Ground it. Give it life.

Give it structure.

Think about what needs to happen next. Think about steps and action plans. Think about strategies and timelines. Build that path, bit by bit. Create that structure for yourself. Do it even if you feel uncomfortable. Even if a part of you is rebelling against that structure.

Do it and you'll find that what you're really creating is freedom. True freedom.

To dive deeper into this topic, download free tools and advanced strategies at www.LiveBigTheBook.com/Tools.

DEATH

BY

DESIRE

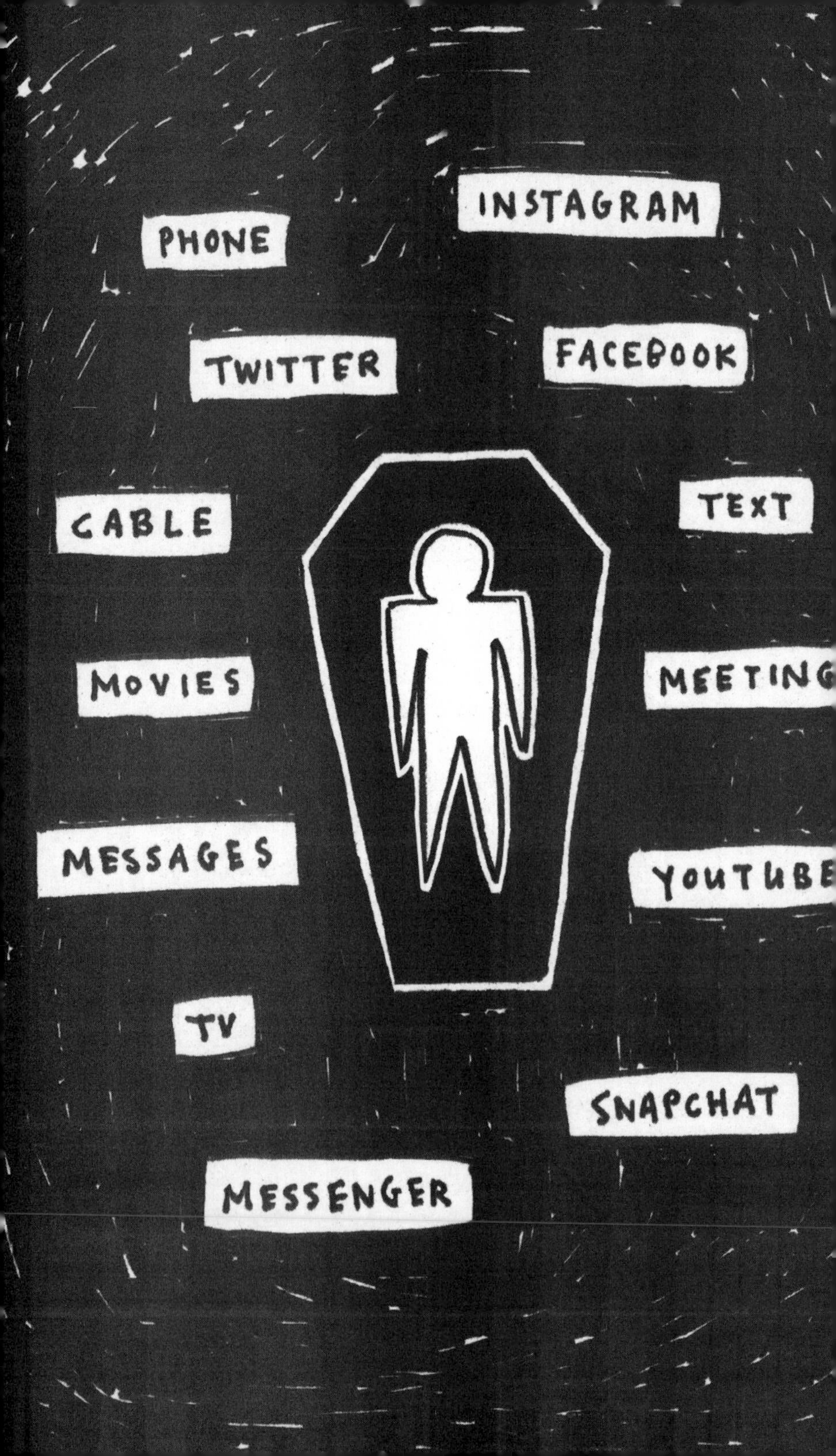

PHONE
INSTAGRAM
TWITTER
FACEBOOK
CABLE
TEXT
MOVIES
MEETING
MESSAGES
YOUTUBE
TV
SNAPCHAT
MESSENGER

CHAPTER 9

Death by Desire

The fear of missing out on things makes you miss out on everything.

—Etty Hillesum

When he was the CEO of Microsoft, Bill Gates used to go on what he called a "think week." These think weeks would go down a couple of times a year. Think weeks were phases of complete isolation, when Gates locked himself away from the outside world. The idea was to get quiet, connect different ideas, and come up with *bigger* ideas and thoughts.

The think weeks soon became legendary not just within Microsoft but for entrepreneurs everywhere. The results he created from ideas he came up with during his time in voluntary isolation altered the trajectory of Microsoft again and again. Some of these ideas changed the world.

It has become increasingly harder for us to create any length of uninterrupted time and space for our thoughts to flow freely and to think creatively about anything. World-changing devices like our smartphones also have the dual role of disrupting our lives. Our overconnected, high-speed, internet-driven world never stops. Ever.

There's always more to see, hear, and do. There are endless messages to read and emails to reply to. There are newsfeeds to check out and posts to scan. We constantly feel that there's always something better, something smarter, something sexier out there. It's at the point where we're drowning in a perpetual feeling of "missing out." This digital phenomenon has a name—Fear of Missing Out or FOMO. Keeping our minds open, clear, and undisturbed is an unattainable dream for most of us, and it's all because of one thing—our own desire.

Our desire to stay connected.

Our desire to constantly check our phones, messages, and emails.

Our desire to share everything and anything.

Our desire to communicate all the time.

Our desire to *know*—that's the most dangerous desire of all.

These desires have become a death trap and they're draining our souls. They're draining us of ideas and inspiration. They're stealing our time and creating empty meaningless moments spent staring at a screen. They're taking away our opportunity to do masterful work. Yes, I know this sounds dramatic, but that's because it is. We're choosing death by desire and this is an issue that's as serious as a heart attack.

When I connect with entrepreneurs around the world, I see more and more heads nodding when I start to talk about social media and how we have all become slaves to it. Maybe you're nodding right now as you read this or maybe you have a resigned look on your face as you shrug your shoulders.

I know you're feeling the pain of this. I know we've collectively presented our souls and our time at the altar of the social media gods—Twitter, Facebook, Instagram, WhatsApp, Snapchat. But here's some good news.

It's *our* desire to know, *our* desire for those dopamine hits we get with likes, shares, and comments, and *our* desire that's holding us in slavery and keeping us tied to these false gods. This means the power to override these desires is in *our* hands. We have the ability to take control. We are the ones who must set ourselves free.

You are the only one who can stop your magical unicorn ideas from dying the sad death of an old, tired donkey in the middle of a desert. Weird image, isn't it? I want you to have that image in your mind the next time you get on Facebook "just for a minute." I want you to think of the dying donkey when you post the picture of your third latte of the day. I want you to hear that donkey bray and I want you to take that as your personal alarm to stop checking social media and start running your business. Dying donkeys braying? I know it's kind of extreme, but this is your life. Those likes and shares are not your reason to live. You are meant for so much more than that.

In his book *Deep Work,* your time spent between work, desires, and distractions is what Cal Newport calls "fractured time." And fractured time is the time you spend trying to do too many things at the same time. You jump from one idea to the next in quick succession. You open and reply to your emails as and when they come in. You are chained not just to one other person's agenda but to *everyone* else's agenda. You are in constant reactive mode. You are in "pleasing everybody" mode. This is the nightmarish reality for most of us. It's crazy but we've done it for so long that it's now the new norm.

But there is a better place. A place where we have the time to think, to reflect, and to reconnect with ourselves. A place of quiet and (usually) of solitude where ideas percolate and arise in a natural flow and we have long periods of undistracted, uninterrupted time to create solid, masterful results.

This place is called "deep work."

Can I just say how much I love deep work? It's saved my ass more times than I can remember. This book exists because I put myself into deep work mode, which means I have eyes only for this book until it's done *(my wife, Neeta, is a writer, too, so luckily for me she understands)*. I don't listen to, watch, or read anything that is not related to this book.

I do this twice a year *(feeling like Bill Gates here . . . just a few billions short).* I go into deep work mode to write books like this one or to just read and create plans for my business in the coming months and years. These are the times I've come up with some of my best, most innovative, transformational ideas. Deep work mode has allowed me to create an incredibly successful business that continues to grow—and that's not even the best part.

I've found deep work can be applied even outside the business space.

I now set aside at least four days where Neeta and I go away together to a gorgeous location. We do this at least once a year—twice, if our schedules allow. We have an unbreakable rule when we plan these yearly getaways: our destination must feature a bad internet connection. I mean *really* bad. Even better if it has no internet connection at all.

During these four days, Neeta and I plan how we can up the game in our relationship and in our marriage. We talk about how we can get things to be sexier, deeper, more powerful, more inspiring and creative, and altogether "awesomer."

These four days are pure magic. Every single time we go away, we come back with renewed faith and love for each other and for all that we bring to our relationship. These breaks bring a new dimension to our relationship. Every. Single. Time. It's the best.

We've talked about a lot of stuff in this chapter. We've talked about donkeys, deserts, and sexier relationships, but I want to go back to that thing we started with:

Your desire to check that message, check that email, check that post puts you in an endless reactive state and your life and business get constricted and confined and ultimately get lost in the shuffle. When all you do is react, you're blocking all of that amazing intuitive inspiration, ideas, and insights that bring life and joy and fun into everything you do.

This is *your* business. This is *your* life.

Don't choose death by desire. You deserve more than that.

To dive deeper into this topic, download free tools and advanced strategies at www.LiveBigTheBook.com/Tools.

ZERO FUCKS GIVEN

CHAPTER 10

ZFG

I have many talents, but giving a fuck is not one of them.

—Unknown

First, SLA: Strong Language Ahead.

Now, ZFG: Zero Fucks Given.

Urban Dictionary explains ZFG as the inability to give even one fuck about someone or something.

Here is the story of an entrepreneur (if you give at least a few fucks):

Giving a fuck about what others think is a mistake.

If you give a fuck about other people's opinions of you, you will never make anything of yourself.

You may think you must give a fuck about what your family thinks, until your business turns into a "success" on some traditional media channel so they can claim their daughter/son/sister/brother/nephew is a somebody.

But actually, you don't.

If you start to give a fuck about what people are saying or whispering or gossiping about you, you'll start to worry about what you've done and what you haven't done.

You'll worry about what is supposedly right and wrong.

You'll wonder if you are good enough.

Smart enough.

Inspiring enough.

And you'll usually come up short.

Because you're giving a fuck about what's going on inside other people's heads.

No one should be giving a fuck about these things. Doesn't matter if you are an entrepreneur or not. Those are fucks that should not be given. When you care about any of the above, you will start to create a reality that doesn't mean anything to you. You will start to create a life and business that is not based on *your* values.

As discussed in *The Subtle Art of Not Giving a Fuck* by Mark Manson, you should work on your art and not give a fuck. You should at least not give a fuck about ideas and people that don't matter to you. Don't matter in the context of your world, your goals, your business.

There are a few things that you *should* care about. I call it the "Give a Fuck" list or the GAF list.

Give a fuck about what your clients experience:

about the good things you are creating in the world

about innovation and bringing about something that is exciting and powerful about having a good time while doing all of this

about connecting with your friends and family

about your health

about your loved ones

about your team

about your surroundings

about nature

about animals

about the planet

about the experiences you create for yourself in this world

about the experiences that you bring to the world.

Give a fuck about *you*.

When we care too much about what someone else thinks, we end up creating a reality from the perspective of the other person. Another person's perspective is just that—a *perspective*. It is not truth. It is not fact. Plus, another person's point of view is based on what they know about you, which is never complete because they are not you. They have a completely different experience of the world.

Trying to live up to other people's ideals and ideas will leave you cold and empty. It will bring up feelings of not "good enough," which comes from doubt, fear, and self-judgment. You might experience loss of power, loss of drive, loss of happiness. You might lose your hair. I can't prove it, but I feel this actually happened to me. I lost all my hair to the Not Good Enough

Disease. So, do a ZFG right now and cure yourself of not good enoughness if only for the sake of your hair.

When you care about things that don't empower you, you simply can't move in the direction you want to because you are held back by those things. You will be caught in a loop. A spiral. You will be running in place. Stuck.

I know this is easier said than done so I'm going to teach you a great hack. If you find yourself starting to care about something that isn't worth a fuck, here's what I want you to do. I want you to use "The Work," which was created by my girl Byron Katie *(I don't know her personally, but I love what she does so much it feels like she's "my" girl, so I'm just going to roll with it).*

The Work sounds hard, but it's simple. It consists of asking yourself just four questions. Do this every time you start giving a fuck about something you shouldn't be giving a fuck about.

Question 1: Is it true? (Yes or no. If no, move to question 3.)

Question 2: Can you absolutely know that it's true? (Yes or no.)

Question 3: How do you react? What happens when you believe that thought?

Question 4: Who would you be without the thought?

I don't want to overstep the line here, and I am by no means an enlightened soul like Byron Katie, but I do want to say this— there's a way you can speed up the process of The Work. You can quickly get out of the funk that comes from giving too many fucks about things that don't matter by keeping your answers to those questions 100 percent honest and truthful. When you do this, you will find yourself skipping the second question. You'll realize that most of what you're thinking and feeling just isn't true.

You will come to see that unhelpful thoughts are generated because of a false belief or incomplete understanding of what others think, feel, and say about us. As you do The Work, it will be clear to you that you don't have to give a fuck about things that don't empower you.

Commit to giving a fuck only about empowering things.

This will probably be the only business book you read that features the word *fuck* so many times in one chapter. Did it make you feel uncomfortable?

I like to practice what I preach, so here's what I say to that: ZFG. Zero Fucks Given.

To dive deeper into this topic, download free tools and advanced strategies at www.LiveBigTheBook.com/Tools.

DON'T BURN YOUR BRIDGES

LEVERAGE MOVES THE WORLD

CHAPTER 11

Don't Burn Your Bridges

*I do not burn bridges. I just loosen the bolts a
little each day.*

—Unknown

Steve Jobs did it.

Jeff Bezos did it.

Mark Zuckerberg did it.

Sara Blakely—who revolutionized pantyhose with Spanx—
did it too.

These entrepreneurs created entire empires from a *single*
idea. They created something so meaningful it reached and
transformed millions of lives.

That single idea changed the world and turned them into
billionaires.

This is the essence of entrepreneurship.

This is who an entrepreneur is.

This is what an entrepreneur does.

There is glory and glamor in it.

There is passion and power behind it.

The call of entrepreneurship is magnetic.

It's an irresistible siren song that ignites a spark that grows into a flame. And it's a flame that burns brighter and with more intensity with every passing day until we pay heed to it. Until, that is, we make that decision to join the prestigious ranks of Jobs, Bezos, Zuckerberg, and Blakely to do it . . .

Become an entrepreneur.

(Cue fireworks, drumroll, running unicorns . . . all of it. Magical!)

So, we plan our steps and we start with the first one: ditch that job. Escape the cubicle. Discard the mindless drudgery of 9 to 5. This was exactly what I did back in June 2008.

It was also the reason why I was drenched in sweat. My shirt sticking to my back. A thin film of perspiration covering my forehead. The tropical heat of Malaysia didn't help matters, and with every minute that passed, I became more and more uncomfortable. I was starting to look like someone had turned a garden hose on me! But I wasn't too worried about how I looked. I had far bigger problems on my mind.

I had just quit my job in a fit of passion. I had no plan. No strategy. No concrete ideas and no funds to support the vague idea I did have. But I was overcome by my desire to become an entrepreneur. Nothing was going to stop me.

So, I handed in my resignation.

(Kaboom! You go, Ajit!)

And I was taken by surprise when I felt afraid instead of inspired.

What had I done?

The rent.

The bills.

How was I going to pay them?

Why hadn't I thought things through?

Suddenly, the glamor of entrepreneurship faded into a dark feeling of panic. This was a mistake. I needed time to plan my exit and transition from full-time employee to self-made boss man. But there was no turning back.

I couldn't go back. My ego wouldn't let me. I was forced to face the future and move forward. There's a long, complex story that takes place between that moment and where I am now, so I'll cut to the chase and give you a quick summary.

My life became hard. *Really hard.*

(Fireworks fade to black. Silence. Unicorns, nowhere to be found.)

At times, it was almost unbearable. Long days and nights at my computer. No weekends. No holidays. Burnout was a constant threat and not being able to pay the bills was an even bigger one. I experienced a roller coaster of emotions—feeling like a success one moment and a failure the next. I had fallen for the romantic notion of being an entrepreneur. I thought it was about taking big leaps of blind faith. I thought entrepreneurship was about risk. The bigger the risk, the bigger the reward.

I was wrong.

I learned much later that the most successful entrepreneurs in the world don't take risks, they *manage* risks, very carefully and very effectively. I realized a little too late that I had learned the wrong thing. I had learned from legendary stories that are repeated as entrepreneurial folklore—about launching your ideas out in the world, guns blazing. I had fallen for the "no guts, no glory" stories of entrepreneurship and I was learning the hard way that there's far more to it than most people will tell you.

So, I'm going to tell you what no one told me.

Entrepreneurship is hard.

Entrepreneurship is pain.

Entrepreneurship is uncertainty.

Entrepreneurship is a lot more working hours than your average 9 to 5.

Entrepreneurship is all of that and more.

If you're ready to quit your job and enter entrepreneurship with the romantic idea I had about it and you jump into the deep end with both feet, hands tied behind your back, blindfolded—without savings or funding, without a plan, without a strategy—do it knowing this.

You are about to enter the most uncertain time of your life. You are giving up your one source of certainty, the single, solid foundation that you have—your job. And while everyone tells you to quit now and do what you love as an entrepreneur, I'm going to tell you to do the opposite.

Wait.

If you don't wait, you're inviting failure, disappointment, heartache, and burnout into your life. It's a guarantee.

If you quit your job because you think you have this one, brilliant idea that everyone's going to fall in love with . . .

If you quit because you want to take a chance on this idea that you have not tested, so you have no clue if it actually resonates with clients and customers . . .

If you quit without a solid plan A backing up that idea and then plans B, C, and D to back up that first strategy if it fails . . .

Then you're in for a freaking high octane, adrenaline pumping, extraordinarily terrifying time.

But you don't have to do it this way.

It's okay to take a leap like this—and fail—when you're twenty or twenty-one or twenty-two. You want to explore and learn more about yourself at that age—who you are and who you are not. You're accumulating knowledge and experiences in your early twenties and that's what you should be doing. That's okay.

It's *not* okay to do the same thing in your thirties and forties and beyond. You have more responsibilities later in life and less time to turn your dreams into reality. So, you need to be single-minded, focused, and strategic in your quest for entrepreneurial glory. You need to find some security. You need to harness stability and strength. You need to ground yourself so you can take the "punches" that are going to come your way as an entrepreneur. And there are going to be plenty of punches.

You see, it's not just the punches known as "low funds" or "inconsistent income" that you'll have to face but also the punch called "no time," the punch called "lack of resources," and the punch called "uncertainty" about your idea and whether it's going to take flight.

These factors are part of the game, and if you have at least one thing that's secure—and that's usually your steady, maybe boring, but reliable job—it creates a strong core foundation. It grounds you and you are able to deflect these punches and fight back.

So, don't quit that job just yet. Don't burn that bridge.

Build on that bridge. Leverage off the job that you have now. Think of it as seed capital for your business and develop your idea and your entrepreneurial skills on the side.

Now that I've scared you, let me share a truth that's going to take the edge off: running your own business is one of the greatest experiences you will ever have in this life.

Entrepreneurship will give you joy.

It will give you purpose.

It will give you flow.

It will give you a chance to be of service.

It will satisfy the deepest parts of your soul, despite all the pain and the heartache.

So, go ahead, and test that idea.

Make it work or have it fail.

Whatever happens, learn what you need to learn and take your next strategic step.

Look first and then leap from that bridge. Just don't burn it.

To dive deeper into this topic, download free tools and advanced strategies at www.LiveBigTheBook.com/Tools.

NO

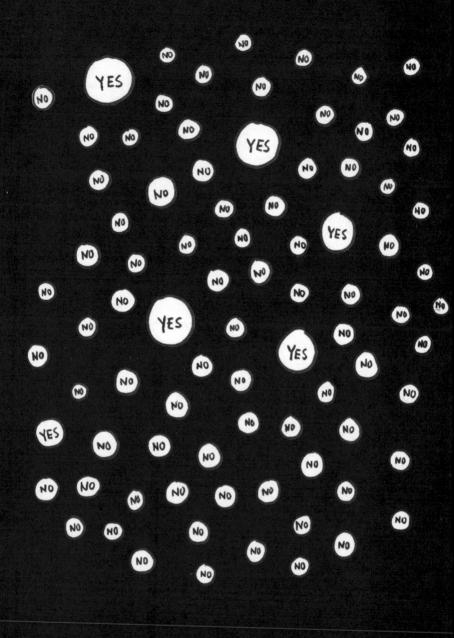

CHAPTER 12

No

Say no to everything so you can say yes to the one thing.

—Richie Norton

"No, I don't want to invest in your company."
"No, this product is not for me."
"No, I don't have the money for this service."
"No, we don't think it's a good business model."
No. That stab of rejection and dejection we feel every single time we hear it. The word that makes us want to quit. The two-letter troublemaker, which early on in business feels like the end of everything. The big scary statement that seems to be about us and how we don't measure up. The word we dread. The word we hate. The word we never want to hear.

This is the word I've come to see as the best word in the world.

I stand by that. It's the best.

If you don't feel like listening to me, at least listen to what Ben Horowitz has to say. He's the cofounder of Andreesen Horowitz, an extremely successful venture capital firm that's invested in some of the world's top tech companies. They are rockstar VC investors, so Horowitz knows what he's talking about. In his book *The Hard Things About Hard Things*, he goes into why no is so much better for business than people think.

It's based on a concept he calls the "market of one." It's a simple idea, but there is genius in its simplicity. When you approach investors, you are not looking for those who will *not* invest in the company. You are looking for "The One" who *will* invest in the company. You are not looking for a bunch of investors; you are looking for just one. You are in the market for just that one sale.

Horowitz captures this idea perfectly here:

> During this time, I learned the most important rule of raising money privately: Look for a market of one. You only need one investor to say yes, so it's best to ignore the other thirty who say "no." We eventually found investors for a series C round (meaning our third round of funding) at an amazing $700 million pre-money valuation and raised $120 million.

The same applies for everything else in business.

When you look for clients, you are not looking for clients who *don't* want your product and service. You are looking for the ones who *do* want your products and services. When you look for team members, you are not looking for people who *are not* passionately interested in what you are trying to create in the world with your business; you are looking for the ones who *are* passionately interested.

You are always in the market of one. One conversation. One conversion. One sale.

These "ones" add up over time. These ones become two and three. A hundred. A thousand. Millions. A billion.

It begins with one, followed by another one.

This is an incredibly powerful idea because when you are in the market of one, you get to protect yourself from the destructive force of hearing "no." You won't feel the rejection and disappointment. No will bother you less and less, even when it comes in big numbers, because you are now focused on looking for the yes.

This attitude and approach works not just in business but in life as well. It filters out all the wrong things and brings through the match that's perfect for you. When I first met Neeta, she explicitly said to me, "I don't date Indian men." It was like a warning. She knew that I was interested in dating her *(I thought I played it cool, but I guess I didn't hide how much I was into her as well as I thought I did)*. She was very clear that I did not pass the "brown, Indian man = good" criterion. *(And just in case you're wondering, Neeta is not racist. She had just come out of a very abusive relationship with an Indian guy, which caused her to reject all Indian men during that period of her life).*

This was a huge problem, of course. I can't help being Indian. I can't wipe the brown off my skin. I can't turn back time and be born into a Caucasian family in the United States. So, I did what I had to do. I accepted her no as a firm no, as any person should. After that initial rejection, I thought I'd rather be Neeta's friend than nothing at all, and so we struck up a friendship.

We would talk until the early hours of the morning about anything and everything. We'd discuss dogmas of religion, our pasts, our futures, our fears, our insecurities, our ambitions, our passions, our sanity, our insanity. We felt comfortable enough to be honest. We were good friends, after all.

I know for a fact that if Neeta had *not* put me in that "no Indian man" category, we wouldn't have had those conversations. We would have held back. We would have been trying to present our "best selves" to each other. We would have put on masks. We would have pursued each other as conquests because that was where we were at that time in our lives. We saw our temporary partners as conquests. Heck, I'm going to go ahead and say it—I was even keeping a count on ethnicities.

But that beautiful, amazing, powerful, incredible "no" that she gave me changed everything for us. It created an intense connection that would have never happened otherwise. Our friendship broke through our carefully put-together personal barriers. It allowed us to move past our emotional and psychological defenses and get to know each other in a real way.

Then, in a far shorter period of time than I could have ever hoped for or even imagined, something amazing happened. As my bud and comedian Hassan Minhaj from the *Daily Show* says, "Once you go brown, you gotta lock that shit down!"

Neeta and I got married. We've been married a total of eight times as I type this sentence. Let me explain: I regularly ask her if she will marry me again. She says yes. Then she jokes that I'm brown, so probably not—and we both end up laughing together. We both know we'll marry each other again for the rest of our lives.

No is magic.

No is power.

The power to know that somewhere deep inside, somewhere down the line, there's a perfect yes that's waiting for you.

To dive deeper into this topic, download free tools and advanced strategies at www.LiveBigTheBook.com/Tools.

OVERNIGHT SUCCESS

OVERNIGHT

10
YEARS
OR
MORE

FEELING
SUCCESS

MASTERY

MARGINAL
GAINS

COMPOUNDING

SUCCESS

CHAPTER 13

How to Become an Overnight Success

*Some say I'm an overnight success. Well, that
was a very long night that lasted about ten years.*

—Lisa Morton

Here's the frustrating part of being an entrepreneur, and
I know it keeps you up at night *(at least some nights)*—
everything takes time!

Building that first product takes time. Getting your team
together takes time. Getting everyone to work together harmo-
niously takes time. Getting that first client takes time. Everything just takes *so much time.*

Why can't it happen faster?

I remember twisting in my chair. You know those incredibly
uncomfortable swivel chairs you see in most offices? I twirled
from right to left and from left to right. It was a habit of mine
back then. I did it when I was thinking hard about something
and I had a lot to think about.

I was twenty-four years old and running a funded startup in India. Facebook was a brand new entity. This was a time when most people thought, "That's a fun online platform! It's the new Myspace!" No one realized at the time just what Facebook would become. How it was about to dominate and change the world. How it would open doors for complete unknowns to become online millionaires.

I had no clue either, but I felt a strange kind of anticipation. It was the feeling I'd had when I watched a movie in the cinema for the first time as a little boy. As I waited for the movie to start, there was a sense of excited anticipation. I knew it was going to be an amazing experience. I just didn't know *how* amazing.

Twisting in that swivel chair, I felt that same sense of excitement. The dawn of the Facebook era marked a new chapter in my life. I knew that instantly. I just didn't know *how* it was all going to go down. I was also thrilled that I'd finally have the chance to show my parents that I wasn't a total disaster and that even though I hadn't graduated from college with a solid, reliable engineering degree that would lead to a solid, reliable job, I could still make something of myself. I could finally prove that I was at least *as good* as my brother and that he was not the only one who was worthy of their pride.

But I wanted all of that instantly. I wanted my bright, successful future to happen now.

Instead, everything was unfolding so slowly and it was driving me up the wall.

Why the heck was it taking so much time? It would take a bunch of failed relationships, countless highs and lows, more failures than I care to remember, and more successes than I could have ever imagined before I finally got the answer to that question.

And during that time *(it took ten long years!)*, I discovered what I like to call the Five Indisputable Laws of Success:

1. The Feeling of Success
2. Ten Years or More
3. Mastery
4. Marginal Gains
5. Compounding

I'm going to share each one of these with you. Let's start with the Feeling of Success.

Most of us never think about what success feels like. We're hyperfocused on what success *looks* like. We chase after this image and we accept it as evidence that we're actually a success in business and in life. This evidence could be anything: a relationship with your dream guy or gal; living in a specific type of home or apartment, such as a mansion or a penthouse; traveling to luxury locations around the world; being friends with celebrities; owning a string of luxury cars; anything that gets you to you tell yourself, "Yeah, I did it. Life is good. I hit the big time. I'm a success!"

This is what we think success *looks* like.

But here's the challenge—our image of success is always measured against external influencers, and this is a dangerous thing. Why? Think about it this way. You're happy about your achievements. You feel good. Then one day, you meet another entrepreneur and they share a part of their story with you—the glorious part, the part where they look like a true hero—and your definition of success starts to shift.

As you listen to their story, you start to forget about everything you've worked so hard to achieve and create. That dreamy person you're dating, that gorgeous house by the beach, that awesome holiday in the Bahamas, they all start to lose their shine.

Suddenly you're not a success if you don't have exactly what that entrepreneur has—this could be a private jet, houses and apartments around the world, a yacht—it doesn't matter. You can't help feeling like your wins are small and insignificant. Disappointment and doubt enter your mind. You start to believe that if your success doesn't look like their success, you're a failure.

But here's something you haven't thought about—you haven't decided what success should *feel* like for you.

You see, most of us build our business while looking over our shoulder at other people's success stories. We want the same story for ourselves. We want the cars other people drive. We want to live in their houses. We want to work with their rockstar team. We want to learn from their mentors, and on and on.

Yet we don't know what it actually *feels* like to walk in their shoes. We know what it *looks* like from the outside, but we don't have the slightest clue about what it *feels* like, and this is the reason why we end up chasing after the wrong thing.

Almost without exception, success looks a certain way and feels like something else.

Success looks sexy. It's like an A-list celebrity: she's always dolled up and smiling or he has a perfect six-pack and a confident look. They're hot, sexy, and so desirable. They look like success. But how do they feel? What's going on in their hearts and minds? Often, they feel alone. They may be hungry for true friendship. They may be longing for true love. They may be feeling judged and they miss their privacy.

I'm not saying you shouldn't chase after the fun, luxurious, beautiful things that come with success. It's okay if success looks like fast cars, fame, and fortune for you, but know this:

The only way to truly achieve success without giving up on your happiness is to understand and define what success needs to *feel* like for you. Not just what it looks like. An image of success isn't enough. You have to go much deeper. You have to explore the emotions and feelings that you want to have. You need to get to the Feeling of Success—the one that's right for you. That's the first Indisputable Law of Success.

Now, here's the second law—Ten Years or More.

My twenty-four-year-old self was focused only on achieving success *right now*. Yet success means nothing if it's fleeting. If it passes you by in an instant. You want success to last far longer than a few weeks or months.

And here's the truth about lasting success—it takes time. It's something that's created one little bit at a time. You start with a small idea. A passion. An interest. As you go through weeks, months, and years, and you stay interested and passionate about that skill or idea, you'll achieve sustainable, lasting success.

Matthew McConaughey, a guy who's no stranger to success, said this in his acceptance speech while receiving his Oscar for Best Actor at the 2014 Academy Awards:

When I was fifteen years old, I have a very important person in my life come to me and say, "Who is your hero?" And I said I don't know, I gotta think about that. Give me a couple of weeks. I come back two weeks later. This person comes up and says, "Who's your hero?" And so I thought about it and I said, you know who it is—it's me in ten years.

So I turn twenty-five. Ten years later that same person comes to me and goes, "So are you a hero?" And I was like, not even close. No, no, no. She said, "Why?" I said because my hero is me at thirty-five.

Think about how things would be ten years from now. How you would want to *feel* ten years from now. Understanding who you want to be ten years from now will give you a view of the world like no other. You can see what needs to happen now for your future self to look and feel like what you truly desire. Having a ten-year version of yourself in your mind's eye gives you a vision to aspire to. To chase.

Your vision will come true. It *will* happen. No question.

On to the third law—mastery.

When you are preparing something, when you are just learning something new, you experience an exponential curve. Your mind is expanding like never before. You are getting constant validation from the outside world about the value of your newly acquired skill.

And then you reach a stage where that curve ends. What you learn then seem marginal. It seems like you already know "that."

Most individuals stop right around there. However, successful entrepreneurs, avid learners, and growth-centered individuals know that they are on track to becoming better—they know they are on track to mastery.

Mastery is a journey to excellence, which is the somewhat perfection of the art you have mastery in. Mastery is where you take something and seem to do little with it, but it creates exponentially better results. Mastery is where exponential growth happens while little effort seems to have been made.

When I started Evercoach, an education and training platform built specifically for coaches, authors, teachers, and speakers, it was a little website with little financial backing. What it *did* have was me, with more than seven years of experience in building education-based businesses. I was closing in on the mastery stage. This meant I could see what educators usually don't see. Now, we are one of the largest, more impactful platforms for coaches online. It took two years. It happened because there was a smudge of mastery that was backing this platform.

Mastery lasts.

The fourth Indisputable Law of Success is Marginal Gains. This is something we hardly notice while it's happening, but it's the secret behind some of the most accomplished people of all time.

Marginal gains is a concept that focuses on this single, simple idea: if you take small, consistent forward movements every day—even if many of these steps feel disconnected—you are making progress that will eventually lead to the creation of something meaningful and powerful.

Let's look at Facebook. Right now, this is a company that pretty much runs the world. It shares public opinion across the planet. We've seen it used, again and again, as a channel to project "the voice of the people." Facebook has played a role in national revolutions. It's influenced political policies. It's even touched on religious issues.

And it all began with Zucknet. Ever heard of it? It was a twelve-year-old Mark Zuckerberg's online program and he created it to support his father's dental practice. When you really think about this, it means Zuckerberg was working on creating technology that connects people since he was twelve. He was making marginal gains over years and years before he finally got to where he is right now.

The late Steve Jobs once said, "You can only connect the dots backwards." You will only know *after* the fact how that little gain that seemed to have nothing to do with your big goals is the thing that tipped the scales in your favor. But you can be sure it will add up over time. It always does. Always.

The final Indisputable Law of Success comes from an unexpected place—the world of finance.

Financial gurus love the concept of compound interest. They absolutely adore it. They can go on and on talking about it—what it does, how it works, and how it can be used to create massive financial gains.

Compound interest, sometimes known as compounding interest, is essentially interest calculated on the initial principal and also on the accumulated interest of previous periods of a deposit or loan.

You can easily apply this principle in business. Our clients compound. Returns on our products compound. Your overall revenue compounds. As the years go by, just by you working on your mastery, just by your marginal gains, your results compound—tremendously.

I've found that doing the work you do in your business for two to three years will yield up to four to five times in returns. Often, returns are much higher than that.

And this brings me back to where we started—the title of this chapter.

How to become an overnight success. Have you figured it out yet?

There are absolutely no overnight successes. Zero.

No one made it without identifying and recognizing what success actually feels like for them, without sticking to it for ten years or more, without mastery, marginal gains, or compounding.

If you think they came out of nowhere and hit the big time in the blink of an eye, it's because you don't know the full story. This backstory is always one of struggle, pain, and hard work, and this is why no one wants to talk about it. It's a story where your hero gets scarred and feels unsure and it is not a sexy story.

It's sexier to say, "I just showed up and success rained down on me."

That has never happened and it will never happen. Ever.

There is no overnight success. Success takes time.

To dive deeper into this topic, download free tools and advanced strategies at www.LiveBigTheBook.com/Tools.

INTUITIVE INTELLI-
GENCE

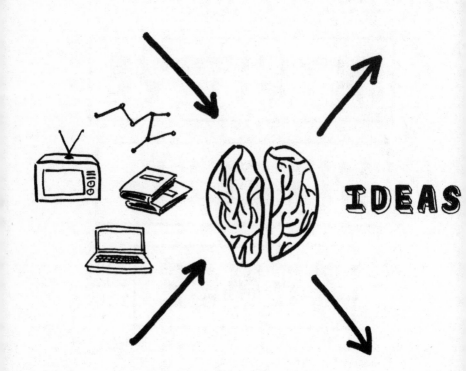

CHAPTER 14

Intuitive Intelligence

The only real valuable thing is intuition.

—Albert Einstein

t was one of the first times I tried to create a proposal for a marketing campaign. I was looking for ideas to jazz things up when a senior person in the company suggested I add the line, "In God we trust, everyone else bring data."

I remember thinking, "This guy's a poet." I was highly impressed with him until I realized that the line wasn't his but actually a quote by W. Edwards Deming, a multitalented man who wore many hats. An engineer, professor, author, management consultant, and award-winning statistician, he is widely recognized as one of the key people who influenced Japan's exponential economic growth in the fifties and sixties.

There is a tremendous amount of truth to Deming's poetic line. I'm not going to say if he was right about God *(that's a conversation I'll reserve for another book)*, but he's spot on with the second half of that quote. Everyone should definitely bring

data. Unfortunately, I know many entrepreneurs who will dis-
agree with that wisdom.

The majority of entrepreneurs I've worked with resist taking a real look at their business to understand how it actually
works. I'm talking about the nuts and bolts that keep it moving
and expanding, the elements that keep it alive and growing.
Getting to know your data is one of the quickest and most
accurate ways to get a clear idea on what's working and what's
not working in a business.

When I try to bring data and numbers into my conversations with entrepreneurs, I usually hear something like this:

"It's way too complex for me, Ajit."

"I'm not a data person."

"Can we please not talk about numbers? I hate numbers."

"Data? How boring!"

These hardworking business owners don't see just how
important data is and how no amount of blood, sweat, and
tears will take the place of the simple act of "knowing your
numbers." They have no idea that data can provide them with
the insights they need to make powerful and precise decisions
in their business. They don't understand that the data they
already have on hand—but are unaware of—can change the
trajectory of their entire business. Most important, they don't
realize that conscious knowledge of all of these details can
bring about unbelievable results and success in strange, and
often unconscious, ways.

Here's an example. I was talking to my wife, Neeta, the
other day. We had just finished hosting a retreat for some of
the most extraordinary entrepreneurs on the planet. We were
already in tremendously high spirits when I received news

that made us feel even more amazing. One of the companies I owned was about to be acquired for an impressive amount of money. We didn't know exactly what the future had in store for that company, but we did know that the corporation that acquired it would work hard to open the door to more success, more opportunities, more expansion, and more revenue.

Neeta and I were ecstatic.

We started talking about our lives and our experiences in business. The ups and downs. Trials and tribulations. Then the conversation took an interesting twist. I'm the founder and the cofounder of a string of companies, and we realized that many of these companies had become extremely successful very, very rapidly. Some of them had been acquired at an incredible price by other successful businesses.

We were determined to discover the framework that consistently created these awesome results. What was happening here? What were the decisions that led repeatedly to phenomenal success? What was I doing differently?

As we took a deep dive into this question, an unusual pattern began to emerge. It was something I hadn't noticed before, and I'd like to warn you now: it's something that may challenge your thinking and even your beliefs.

Let me explain. A big chunk of my working hours is spent on research and study. I look at data and I read a lot. But I also do a ton of deep thinking and reflection on why and how something works. This process always gives me interesting ideas and creates clarity around the topic.

Now, you might think that all this research and study followed by deep thinking will naturally lead to rational, clear decisions and you'd be right.

Except that my decisions are rarely accepted as rational *by other people.*

Those who know me think of me as an analytical person and they are repeatedly shocked at how "illogical" my decisions seem to be. My mother always seems to be the most surprised. When I was on track to get a significant promotion at my first job, I decided to quit. It made no sense to her. Why would anyone quit a well-paying job at twenty-four? Most young professionals would be holding on to it tightly. I did so because I knew that although I would have done well at that job had I kept it, I would miss the opportunity of the internet that was coming up.

My mother thought I was losing my mind.

This isn't unusual.

Entrepreneurs who aren't afraid to push past their comfort zone and think way outside the box are often laughed at or accused of being crazy. At least at first. Then, much to everyone's amazement, they go on to achieve incredible success. These entrepreneurs seem to have Lady Luck on their side. They navigate past obstacles and challenges with ease. They make incredibly perceptive decisions. Eventually everyone applauds and calls them a genius.

What's their secret? *Intuitive intelligence.*

We all have a conscious mind and a subconscious mind. The conscious mind is the part of your mind that's in the driver's seat. This is the part of you that's awake and alert. When we're aware of what's going on inside our heads, it's the conscious mind that holds this awareness. This is where we rationalize and analyze. This is where we process our conscious thoughts, our feelings, and so forth.

Next, we have the subconscious mind, which, when you realize its power, makes your conscious mind seem small and weak. There's almost no limit to what your subconscious mind can do. It's even more powerful than a supercomputer. It takes in data—and I mean *all* the data—about everything. It has the ability to absorb and process every little detail of what's happening around you at every second, but you are completely unaware of this immense amount of background data as it filters through into your conscious mind.

Scientists have yet to agree on an exact number, but it is believed that our subconscious mind processes millions of bits of information per second. *Per second.* The power of your subconscious mind is incomprehensible. Personally, I think of the subconscious mind as a massive data storage unit that captures everything, without filters, and I think of the conscious mind as the command center that can retrieve specific information from this immeasurably vast storage space.

Right now, there is significantly more happening in your mind as you read this than you are even aware of. There is an ocean of information entering your brain—the smells, the sounds, the sights, the touch—while your focus and awareness remain on these words.

Your subconscious is doing all the work. It's processing data in the background while your conscious mind does one thing—understand these words. If you want to, you can easily shift your attention to something else that's going on around you in less than a microsecond. This is because that data is already inside your brain. It was invited in by your subconscious. You are simply bringing that data up to your conscious awareness.

How does all of this tie into your business? Well, it means you know everything there is to know about everything in your business. You know everything about what's right and what's wrong for your business. Far more than you *think* you know. Far more than you can rationalize.

To put it another way—you're a freaking genius. The problem here is that you don't realize just how much of a genius you are and most of us have no clue how to connect into our own genius to create the outcomes we want. We block the connection between the subconscious mind and the conscious mind. This connection has a name and it's something you've heard of before—intuition.

When you know how to work with your intuition, you'll start to make choices and decisions that go way beyond anything your conscious mind can possibly decipher because your intuition connects your conscious awareness to the much larger data set that resides in your subconscious.

And that's not even the best part. Your intuition works in an instant. It usually shows up as a *feeling,* an *epiphany,* or an *insight.* It's incredibly efficient and radically more effective than conscious thought. That feeling that came up out of nowhere, that insight that you seem to understand even without reflecting on it—that is your intuitive intelligence at work.

Advertising tycoon and marketing genius David Ogilvy was talking about intuitive intelligence in his book *Ogilvy on Advertising* when he said:

> Big ideas come from the unconscious. This is true in art, in science, and in advertising. But your unconscious has to be well informed, or your idea will be irrelevant. Stuff

your conscious mind with information, then unhook
your rational thought process. You can help this process
along by going for a long walk, or taking a hot bath, or
drinking half a pint of claret. Suddenly, if the telephone
line from your unconscious is open, a big idea wells up
within you.

Notice Ogilvy says "stuff your conscious mind with information." That's a critical part of the process of working with
intuitive intelligence. This is where knowing your data, crunch-
ing numbers, thinking about how things work, come in. But
most entrepreneurs stop there. They read and they rationalize
and they think and they analyze. Then they make a decision.
Big mistake.

Yes, of course it's important to rationalize and to analyze.
It's important to consciously focus on what you are working
on and look for relevant information before you make major
decisions in your business. There's no question about that. But
listening to your intuition, listening to that insight you receive
out of the blue—that's a much more powerful approach.

I've discovered that my intuitive intelligence comes through
loud and clear during two very specific experiences:

1. When I am in a state of meditation
2. When I operate from a place of love

Sounds mushy and a bit "woo woo," I know, but it's true
for me. It could be different for you. You need to experiment
with this process for yourself to find out what works so you
can start to tap into your intuitive intelligence. You might feel

like everything I'm saying here is a bit of a stretch and a little too "out there," but I know as you read this, some part of you knows what I'm saying is true. You're just trying to find a way to rationalize it. That's like trying to crunch data that requires 530,000 KB on an inadequate 53 KB of RAM.

Give it up because that's never going to happen.

Trust me on this one.

Forget what you think you know and embrace what works. Find a way to tune in to a place of love and you'll find the way to tune in to your personal supercomputer.

Your intuitive intelligence.

To dive deeper into this topic, download free tools and advanced strategies at www.LiveBigTheBook.com/Tools.

PART 3

Magic

HOME TEAM = FAMILY

CHAPTER 15

Home Team

You don't build a business, you build people—and then people build the business.

—Zig Ziglar

love comic books. As a kid, I couldn't get enough of India's version of caped crusaders and superhero vigilantes. But when I was growing up, only the "nerdy" kids read comics and that's just how it was.

How times have changed.

Unless you've been living on a planet on the outer rims of the galaxy, you've probably heard of Marvel Comics by now and I bet you can identify at least three Marvel characters. Maybe Iron Man in his cool gold and red suit or Spider-Man in red, blue, and black. Maybe the giant green Hulk comes to mind or Captain America, the do-gooder. Over the years, Marvel Comics has created some pretty bizarre, fascinating storylines for its superhero population, but I think the most interesting story of all is the story of Marvel itself.

At first Marvel wasn't even about comics. The company started out as a magazine publisher but moved into comics in the late 1930s. It did okay for a few decades, but things really started to heat up in the 1960s when the then-young writer-editor Stan Lee entered the scene. Lee decided to shake things up a bit. He worked on storylines that would appeal to children as well as adults, and that's when things began to skyrocket for Marvel.

By the seventies and eighties, Marvel was a phenomenal success and the undisputable king of the comic book industry. Lee and his rockstar team of creatives kept coming up with better and better storylines and creative ideas. They were unstoppable. Marvel was all the rage and their comic books turned into opportunities for speculation and investment. The first issue of a Marvel comic would sometimes fetch over $40,000.

It was crazy, but it was fun.

The company continued to attract the best of the best writers, artists, and editors. This was no surprise, because it was a great place to work. There was creativity and excitement in the air. The team loved what they did. They loved the characters they created. They loved their company.

It looked like Marvel was flying high and nothing could ever bring it down, but as Spider-Man's Uncle Ben says, "With great power comes great responsibility."

When a new owner took over the operations of the company, he immediately looked at ways to up the profits. This guy understood very little about comics. He didn't make the effort to get to know the incredible products or the genius team that created them.

Pressure started to rise.

There was an endless race to increase the bottom line and create more and more profits. The core team of creatives began to feel the pain of this more than anyone else. They felt called to do the work they were inspired to do, but they felt stuck. The constant push for profits over products created an unbearable environment. So, they did the only thing they felt they could do—they walked away from the company they loved so much. The company they had helped to turn into a mega success.

This was 1992.

Just one year after the creative team stormed out, Marvel started to tank. By 1996, the company had to declare bankruptcy. It looked like it was all over for Marvel, but then a new CEO stepped in. He was a man who understood the true dynamics of building a successful company that lasts.

Peter Cuneo's first act was to bring back the original creative team. It was the best decision he could have ever made. In 2009, Marvel was purchased by Disney for $4 billion.

The difference between a company that limps along before it finally dies and a company that continues to flourish and thrive is what I like to call the "Home Team." This is the core team that breathes life into everything in a business. They give their heart and their soul to create products and services that are innovative and that make a difference. They are committed to what they do. They agree with the philosophies and values that drive the business.

They are believers.

The Home Team has the power to make or break a company, and this power usually lies in the hands of a very small group of people. This is true in every kind of company, in every industry imaginable. It's true even in the financial world, which is famous for operating on a hardcore "take no prisoners" and "each person for themselves" attitude.

Here's an example: Warren Buffett is considered by many to be *the* most successful investor of all time. His holding company, Berkshire Hathaway, owns top brands such as Dairy Queen and Heinz Ketchup and employs more than 360,000 people around the world. Guess how many people are on Buffett's Home Team? Twenty-five. Buffett captured just how amazing his team is in an annual letter to his shareholders in 2015:

> This group efficiently deals with a multitude of SEC and other regulatory requirements, files a 30,400-page Federal income tax return—that's up 6,000 pages from the prior year!—oversees the filing of 3,530 state tax returns, responds to countless shareholder and media inquiries, gets out the annual report, prepares for the country's largest annual meeting, coordinates the Board's activities, fact-checks this letter—and the list goes on and on.

Twenty-five people do all that. It's mind blowing.

There is no limit to what a small group of intelligent, dedicated people can do for a company. I know this from personal experience. The truth is there would be no business for me to run without my Home Team. At interviews, I'm often asked, "Ajit, what would you tell your younger self about business?" My answer has been and always will be this: "Your team is there *not* just to perform tasks and do what you tell them to do. They are your Home Team. They are family. They are there to help build a life with you."

Twentieth-century business principles and practices have led us to believe that employees are supposed to crank out tasks in exchange for money. This is an extremely old-fashioned, short-sighted, and inaccurate view. Yes, your team needs to perform tasks, of course. Every task has its place in a business. Tasks are important, but they're not everything. They're not even half of what's needed. Getting tasks done is just a small part of what a Home Team actually does for your company and for you.

Think about your house and your family. There's probably someone who's mainly responsible for cooking the meals. Someone is in charge of getting the lawn mowed. A third person might have to take out the trash each night.

We all have roles in a family, but do you see your family members as task machines? Do you see your brother as the "Trash Collector" or your dad as "The Gardener" or your mom as "The Cook"? They are far more than their roles. They are your family. You love them. You want what's best for them. The tasks need to be done but that's just a small part of the story.

Your Home Team at work is the same. Yes, they need to complete their assigned tasks, but they are greater than the sum of those tasks. They are the team you rely on. The ones who have your back. The ones you can turn to when you're in a jam and need support. I hope I have my Home Team with me for life. These are the people I love. I want to watch them grow and evolve. I want to help them grow and evolve. I want to see them do better and better not just for the company but in their own lives. This is what I want for my wife, my parents, and my future kids.

The one lesson I have learned that will stick with me forever is to build a team for life. Keep these family members for life. Yes, they will quit. Yes, they will get mad at you. Yes, they will think you're unfair or short-sighted or just plain annoying. But that's exactly what happens in a family too. We forgive our family. When they walk away and come back to you, we greet them with open arms.

Thinking of my Home Team as family gives me the direction, purpose, and clarity I need to show up in a way that will help us all rise to the top. I know what I need to do to bring out the best in myself and in every team member because our relationship arises from mutual love, respect, and trust.

We share a bond that transcends business.

This has created incredible opportunities for me to achieve far more than I ever thought was possible. I've been able to cocreate successful businesses with my Home Team. I've been able to hit goals I would never have hit on my own. I've been able to let them go with an open heart when they needed to leave, and bring them back when I was ready for them.

I know my Home Team is there for me and I hope they know I'm there for them even if we're no longer working together.

I want my Home Team.

I need my Home Team.

I love my Home Team.

And so, I reward my Home Team again and again.

This creates a virtuous cycle of love, support, and growth, which leads to long-term prosperity and cash flow. What's the best part?

We do it all because we want to and not because we have to. We do it all because we want the best for each other. Because that's what family does.

To dive deeper into this topic, download free tools and advanced strategies at www.LiveBigTheBook.com/Tools.

...BUT LET THEM GO

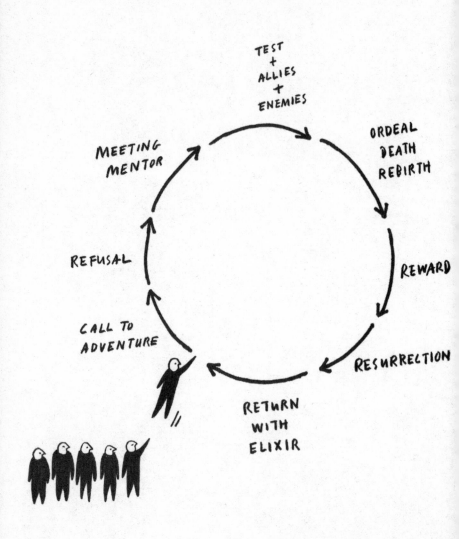

TEST
+
ALLIES
+
ENEMIES

MEETING
MENTOR

ORDEAL
DEATH
REBIRTH

REFUSAL

REWARD

CALL TO
ADVENTURE

RESURRECTION

RETURN
WITH
ELIXIR

* COURTESY : HERO'S JOURNEY BY
* INSPIRED BY: JOSEPH CAMPBELL

CHAPTER 16

. . . But Let Them Go

Some people believe holding on and hanging in there are signs of great strength. However, there are times when it takes much more strength to know when to let go . . ."

—Ann Landers

When I started Evercoach, Aarzoo was the second person to join the team. She's smart as a whip. Driven. Passionate. She's exactly what I think an ideal team member should be. She was the one who figured out an awesome Facebook strategy that attracted countless people to our page. She was the one who created a niche that was strong enough to propel Evercoach to the top. She was pivotal in turning Evercoach into the force that it is now in the coaching space. Then she left.

I was crushed.

In his 1949 book *The Hero with a Thousand Faces*, American scholar and mythologist Joseph Campbell first introduced a conceptual narrative called the Hero's Journey. According to Campbell, important myths from around the world all share a fundamental structure: "A hero ventures forth from the world of common day into a region of supernatural wonder (*x*): fabulous forces are there encountered and a decisive victory is won (*y*): the hero comes back from this mysterious adventure with the power to bestow boons on his fellow man (*z*)."

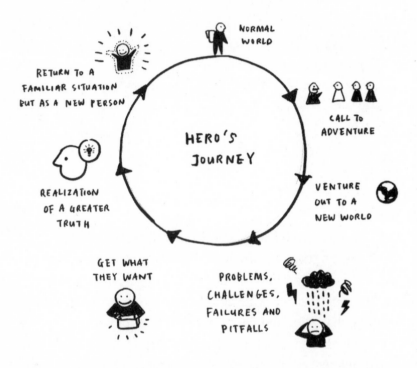

This is essentially the story of how a hero comes into being. Personally, I see the Hero's Journey not so much as the *creation* of a hero but as the *evolution* of a human being. It's the human story and it's a story we all experience.

Here's the thing about people—we are born to grow and to change. When you have gifted, driven team members who understand this truth, you'll notice something interesting. The most brilliant people are the ones who will demonstrate the highest level of discontent.

Don't get me wrong. I'm not saying you're going to discover that your most talented team members are unhappy, frustrated, negative people who love to whine and complain: that's not true at all. My most talented team members are also some of the most positive people I know. What I'm saying is that you're likely to notice an undercurrent of discontent *within* them. This arises from knowing they can do more, that they can be better than they are now. There is something within smart, gifted people that tells them they are meant to live a big, expansive life.

And they love knowing this. They love knowing there is a bright future waiting for them. Most important, they understand that it's not a future that is *given* to them just because they are talented, ambitious, and brilliant. They know they must work for it. They know they must go out into the world and try new things to achieve it.

And this kickstarts the search:

The search for something more challenging.

Something more fun.

Something more exciting.

Something more transformational.

They are constantly dealing with an inner struggle between what is and what could be: between being and becoming.

This struggle makes them the best kind of individual to have on your Home Team.

They know who they are. They know their strengths. They know how to expand into their highest potential. This gives them great energy, great drive. They will do more than you expect them to. They will even push you to be a better version of yourself.

Score!

But that internal struggle that they constantly grapple with will also drive them to seek constant growth. If they wake up enough times not loving what they do, if they don't feel they are growing, if they start to wonder, "What if . . ." too many times, they'll move on. You'll want to hold on to them . . . but you need to let them go.

This is not about you. It's about their lives. Their happiness. Their growth.

They need to leave you to find their next challenge. They need to take a chance, to take a risk to explore new territory.

You'll want to hold onto them . . . but you need to let them go.

I won't lie. It's going be hard. Really hard.

Letting go of a rockstar team player, a friend, a confidante, someone you can rely on, someone who wants you to get to the top and who'll give you their all so you can get there—it's never easy to let go of someone like that. When someone on your Home Team gets ready to leave home, all that drama that comes with being part of a family will come up to the surface.

It will feel that everything will fall apart if they leave you.

You will feel betrayed for a while.

You might even feel you're a bad leader. That they're leaving because you did a bad job.

You didn't.

But you'll want to hold on to them. Don't.

Let them go.

Aarzoo left Evercoach. She embarked on her own journey. She followed her own path and found new adventures—and someday she will come back. She is in my Home Team.

Having your Home Team member leave is like having your beloved child leave home to go to college. Your heart misses them, but you know it's good for them and for the family.

And so, you let them go.

It's the same here. Let your Home Team follow the callings of their heart. Let them grow. Show them kindness and understanding, because it's really hard to leave the people you love and find your own way. It's also hard for them to tell you they're leaving, so don't make it more difficult than it already is.

Sometimes letting go is the best way to support someone and to express love for them. Letting go is the best way to encourage them and to give them room to follow their dreams. Let them go knowing that you'll be there to catch them if they fall. You'll be there when they come back—*if* they come back. Be there for them if they want to go. Be there for them *after* they're gone. Check in and see how they are doing, just like you would with a family member.

Building a good company—a great company—is about being there for your people because that's what it all comes down to.

People. *Your people.*

To dive deeper into this topic, download free tools and advanced strategies at www.LiveBigTheBook.com/Tools.

CULTURE

OF

HAPPI-

NESS

CHAPTER 17

The Culture of Happiness

When the culture is strong, you can trust
everyone to do the right thing.

—Brian Chesky

M y early education in company culture and why it can make
or break a company's future happened back at the start of
my journey in the working world. I was with an organization
called AIESEC. It's the largest not-for-profit, youth organization on the planet. It has about 70,000 members and a strong
presence in 127 countries. AIESEC changes its entire leadership *every year.*

To understand the gravity of this level of upheaval at the
leadership level, think about it this way:

A bunch of sixteen- to twenty-four-year-olds *(this is the
demographic you can't even get to focus on anything more than
the last Instagram post)* come together, discuss who deserves
to be on their leadership team, and then democratically decide
who their new leadership team will be. This has been happening

at the city, country, and international level every year for the past sixty plus years.

Fascinating, isn't it? We as adults find it almost impossible to adjust if we have a new midlevel manager to deal with every three or five years. So, how does this youth-run organization do it? In a word, *culture*.

They have an incredible culture. I was in the AIESEC at the city office and national office in India for four years, and here are five incredibly important things I learned about company culture.

First, the culture is about people.

People create the culture of your company. Heck, they *are* the culture of your company. This means every single person on the team, every single person you hire is an *equal* contributor to the company culture: not less or more, equal. Specific, individual roles don't really matter. It doesn't matter if you're the team leader or if you're the newbie. You are an intrinsic, equal part of the company culture.

When I was in AIESEC, I was the leader of our city chapter. At the time, I had very little experience and even less knowledge about the dynamics of how a company culture works. There were eight individuals on my team at that time. I considered all of them to be my Home Team except for one person. This guy was a highly talented individual but he was also a total menace. He was often late to meetings. He showed frequent displays of aggression and anger. He would get outrageously drunk at parties and belittle other team members.

Here's the conundrum—he was an ace performer. He crushed all his goals. But he was killing team morale and running my patience dry. He didn't fit into the company culture.

Things quickly came to a head and I was ready to fire him. To my surprise, the Home Team stepped in. They spoke up for him. They convinced me to give him another chance. They saved him. After that, he changed. He got better. He made it a point to understand the company culture and work accordingly. And he became a great contributor.

The second thing I learned about company culture—it's everything.

The reason I was so ready to fire this guy is because I felt we wouldn't hit our annual goals with him as part of the team, and I wasn't going to let that happen. AIESEC meant the world to me at that time. It was the only thing in my life that gave me hope that I wouldn't end up an utter disappointment to everyone who knew me. It was the only thing that stopped me from seeing myself as a total failure. But after this individual was saved from being fired, after he changed, things changed for the better for all of us.

We became more certain and even more driven than we already were. We won countless awards that year, including the best AIESEC city office in the country. If even a single individual is out of sync with the company culture, things break apart. But when everyone is in sync, things move forward perfectly. Company culture is like a house of cards. When one card is misaligned, everything falls. It is imperative for the entire team or the company as a whole and for the individual as well to stay aligned with the company culture. Culture is everything.

The third thing I learned—culture is a living organism. It evolves.

The attachment we have to what is and what has been can destroy an organization. As more people get on your team, as you bring in new energies, new insights, new products and services, the culture starts to reshape itself.

This cultural reshaping is a good thing because a fresh, updated culture provides new ideas. It's a fertile field for innovation. You'll discover better systems and processes. Better ways to operate and to communicate. New people also enter the game with new values and beliefs that will add to the mix and create a stronger collective.

Until very recently company culture was thought to be a purely face-to-face, "in the same room," type of thing, but now it's gone virtual. One of my clients has a company with eighty employees. Only fifteen of them live in the same country as he does. The other sixty-five are scattered across the world. It didn't start out that way but my client's company evolved, and so did the culture.

The fourth thing I learned—you need leaders in a culture.

In his book *Hit Refresh*, Satya Nadella states that the C in CEO should stand for *culture*. I couldn't agree more. While it's true that the company culture is created by the people in it, you need a spark to start it all. An igniter. An instigator. A protector.

Let's use the other type of culture as an example—if you want milk to turn into yogurt, you need to bring in a "starter agent" that will transform the milk into yogurt. As the leader of your business, you are like that starter agent. If you don't start the conversation on culture, transformation and creation cannot take place.

The final point I want to emphasize about company culture—values and vision attract the right people and these people will go on to create the perfect culture.

A company's culture is essentially our values and visions coming together to create a unique environment where those values and visions can flourish and thrive. You can't have the chicken without the egg and the egg without the chicken. You can't have a great company culture without great people or great people without a great company culture.

A culture comes together because you set an aspiring vision and values that allow the company to grow, expand, and create great things in the world. This vision along with the set of values are the elements that attract the right type of talent to the company. This in turn will create a culture that will embody those values and vision and expand on them. Without a clear company culture, all you have is a shell. You have an organization that keeps going through the motions but with no heart, no soul, no real motivation for anyone to stay.

But when you have a great culture, anything is possible.

A great culture will drive innovation and create inspiration. It will motivate people to go the extra mile and then a hundred more. It will support your Home Team to go out and achieve more than they ever thought they could. They will bring impossible dreams to reality. They will perform godlike feats. A great culture leads to fulfillment and happiness in the workplace. It's not money or big goals that will do this. It's culture.

When you're building the business of your dreams, follow this rule:

Culture first. People first.

To dive deeper into this topic, download free tools and advanced strategies at www.LiveBigTheBook.com/Tools.

LEADER

OF

NONE

CHAPTER 18

Leader of None

Leadership is not about a title or a designation.
It's about impact, influence, and inspiration.

—Robin Sharma

This may sound a little "cultish," but I'm going to go ahead and share because it's one of my greatest memories as a leader.

It happened when I was leading the city chapter of AIESEC in India, a global young leadership organization, which I mentioned briefly in the previous chapter. It was the final local conference of the year and the highlight of the evening was the closing presentation and intention for the last thirty days of the year. This is when you look back and talk about the previous 335 days of the year. The struggles. The growth. The wins. The losses. It was a very cold night on the outskirts of Jaipur, India. It was bone-chilling, to be honest, and I am not a big fan of the cold. It only made me feel more nervous and my time on stage was approaching fast. My presentation was to begin at 6 PM that evening.

In my heart, I knew this was going to be a night to remember. It was a night of celebration. I was going to replay a video presentation that had won me the election for president of the city chapter. I was feeling nervous and I needed a pick-me-up before I stepped into the spotlight, so I poured myself a quick drink. A few of my team members joined me. We laughed, exchanging memories, remembering the fun times we'd had throughout the year. I started to relax.

We were so excited and when I think back now, we were still kids. None of us was older than twenty-four. I started walking toward the conference room, and as I got closer I realized it was completely dark. Did they forget about the session? Damn! Was there a power failure? I was worried. My nervousness came back. My heart was racing.

I could hear murmurs in the dark but I couldn't see a thing.

I opened the door. The blaring soundtrack from my video from the election started to play. The room lit up. I saw everyone. They weren't sitting down. They were standing on their chairs. They were cheering and clapping . . .

For me.

Tears started rolling down my cheeks.

People continued to cheer.

I couldn't stop crying. My team couldn't stop crying. We made a circle, all of us bawling our eyes out.

I couldn't see through my tears.

For the next forty-five minutes, every single person in the room came together as one. It was supposed to be my night, but we celebrated together as one. I will never forget that experience. Don't get me wrong . . . when I was cheered on like some kind of rockstar, I loved it, every second of it. But I felt strongly that the limelight wasn't just for me. The limelight was for all of us.

That's how I lead.

Many other AIESEC local chapter presidents were happy to take center stage. They were happy to sit in the front row. They gave inspiring closing speeches. They received the accolades and the toasts. But when it was my turn, I made sure my team was standing right there next to me. I wanted my team to be in the front row.

They deserved the rewards. The praise. The accolades.

I may have been their chosen leader, and to the outside world that's what I was. But in my heart I knew the truth. I was only as good as my team. I wouldn't be there without my team.

In reality, I am the leader of none.

I practice this principle to this day. Most people don't know I'm a stakeholder of a number of very successful companies, because I don't go announcing it to everyone I meet. You won't catch me talking about what I had for lunch on Facebook. I rarely jump into the spotlight and people usually have to convince me to take credit for something.

I feel there is one element of leadership that has been ignored for too long. A very important element: great leaders lead by *not* doing much. Great leaders are masterful because they don't get in the way. They don't interfere. When you step away from your ego and you release your competitive streak, you become nicer, better, and more effective. When you don't force your ideas on everyone else, when you don't force a direction, magical things happen.

Your team comes together. They come up with amazing ideas. They set the direction and they are inspired to follow it. They try harder. They do more. And this can only happen when there is no interference and disruption from an egotistical leader who loves hearing his own voice. It seems like a counterintuitive concept for leadership, I know. But I can tell you it works. It's worked for me for more than ten years now, and it seems to work for English film director Guy Ritchie.

Ritchie is behind critically acclaimed movies such as *Lock, Stock and Two Smoking Barrels* (1998) and *Snatch* (2000). He has legions of fans and possibly the most well-known among them is Robert Downey Jr. In an *Off Camera with Sam Jones* interview on YouTube, Downey talks about reading a book called the *Tao of Leadership* when he recognized the importance of being the kind of leader who does nothing at times. A leader who succeeds by not trying to make things happen.

Downey names Ritchie, who was his director in the *Sherlock Holmes* movies, as a great example of this type of leadership. He explains how Ritchie is a master at creating a sense of relaxation and openness on his movie set in a way that allows others to step up and shine. Downey says, "He winds up getting the kind of result he wants by letting things happen."

It may seem uncomfortable, counterintuitive, even threatening to lead from the shadows. There is power in letting the team be. Letting your team create and grow.

So, let's say this:

Be okay with not being in the spotlight.

Be okay with not getting all the credit.

Know that leadership is not about you but about them—your people, your team.

The truth is you can become a world class leader by doing less, not more:

by not doing anything much

by letting others shine

by letting things happen

By being a leader of none.

To dive deeper into this topic, download free tools and advanced strategies at www.LiveBigTheBook.com/Tools.

BALANCE

THE

FORCE

WEAKNESS

VISION
PURPOSE
BRANDING
MARKETING
NEW CREATION
CREATIVITY

FINANCES
HUMAN RESOURCES
SYSTEMS
PROCESSES
STRUCTURE
OPERATION

WEAKNESS

BALANCE THE FORCE

CHAPTER 19

Balance the Force

Focus on being balanced—success is balance.

—Laila Ali

You had an idea. A vision.

This idea, this vision, got you to start your business. You took the company from nothing to where you are now. You drove your company to a profitable place. You hired your first few team members. You worked your ass off nights and weekends.

You started to see results and you were thrilled.

Now you have a different challenge. Now that you have more team members, fundamental elements like good communication seem to be falling apart. Things feel overwhelming, exhausting, daunting.

Most entrepreneurs live from their heads and from their hearts. They have a big vision they aspire to bring to reality. They have goals and dreams. They have enough creativity and drive to take them through the first years of the business. As the business grows, there are more and more processes to follow.

There are systems to set up. There are the day-to-day operations, details, and minutiae to look into. These were never your focus or your interest. You know you need to do these things for the company and you also know you don't like doing them.

You're happy to stick with the 30,000-foot view of your business. You don't really want to come down to earth and work on the little things. You just can't find the patience or get to the right mind-set to do them. These things feel dry and mundane to you. They suck all the energy out of you. Your personal energy—the force within you that brought the company this far—may have diminished or even disappeared.

Is this it? Does this mean this is as far as you go? Is it time to stop?

No, it's not really time to stop, but it *is* time to get support. It's time to start looking to your Home Team as a support system for your business. It's time to put systems and processes in place. It's time for your company to be fueled by a joint force and not just the singular brute force that comes only from you.

This is where you bring balance to the force.

Let me illustrate this with a story about Ray Kroc, the founder of McDonald's. I'll warn you now that there's a lot about Kroc that's not all-inspiring for a heart-centered entrepreneur. There is a dark side to how McDonald's came to be what it is today and some of Kroc's decisions are questionable. But there's also a lot that you can learn from his story, and that's what I'm going to talk about here.

When the McDonald's franchise model started to boom, there were a couple of big challenges that came up. For one thing, when Kroc sold the franchise rights and other McDonald's restaurants opened, the franchisees started messing with the menu. They added food and drink items that were not on the original, approved menu. They started serving burgers that were not up to McDonald's strict standards. Basically, the brand was going to hell in a handbasket because of franchisee noncompliance to standards.

Second, Kroc didn't own McDonald's. He was just the guy who created the franchise model for the company. This meant he couldn't legally make changes to the business. Kroc had to get permission from the owners who regularly disagreed with him. He had a great business model that was working. Kroc was the visionary who made the business successful. He had the drive but he didn't have the strategy to make it profitable and scalable. He was running into scary amounts of debt. He didn't know how to get people to comply with the standards he'd laid down.

Harry Sonneborn was a fan of McDonald's and he learned about Kroc's struggles. He showed Kroc how to control the franchise and how to scale the company. You see, here's the secret behind the company's incredible rise—McDonald's is not a burger joint. It's a real estate company and it was Sonneborn who showed Kroc how to turn McDonald's into a real estate giant. *(If you're thinking, "What?! McDonald's is a real estate company?" just watch* The Founder (2016) *on Netflix and you'll know.)*

Business boomed and with control over the franchise and a more profitable menu, McDonald's became unstoppable. The company now generates more than $64 billion in sales every year *(while ruining people's health—but that's for a whole other book).*

Kroc and Sonneborn were the perfect partners. One was a visionary and the other knew how to transform that vision into reality. Most companies reach a point and go no further because no one knows how to set up structures and pillars to bring a vision into reality. So, you need to balance the force. Sometimes this "balance" comes from just one person, but sometimes it's a team.

That's why you need to discover what your personal force is. What is it that you are really good at doing? What is it that brings out your best? What can you bring to the table that no one else can?

Then look at what the business needs that you *can't* provide.

What are your weaknesses?

What are the things that bore you?

What are the elements that you can't understand?

Identify those. Once you know what they are, find the solution—a person or a group of people. Partner up with them or give them strong roles in the company. Know that the real force that will propel your company, that will skyrocket your profits, is a *combination* of talents, gifts, and skills.

Build the force by hiring or partnering with those who can complement your skills. That's how you nurture the force. That's how you grow the force. That's how you channel the force . . .

By bringing balance to it.

To dive deeper into this topic, download free tools and advanced strategies at www.LiveBigTheBook.com/Tools.

PEOPLE

&

THEIR

PROBLEMS

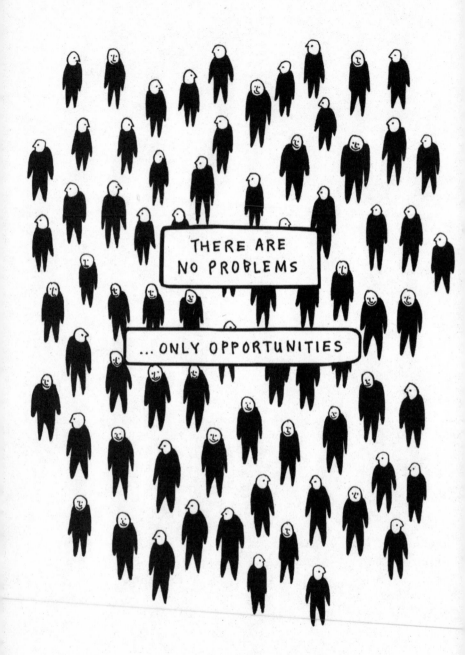

CHAPTER 20

People and Their Problems

Inside of every problem lies an opportunity.

—Robert Kiyosaki

I had a challenge with my mother a few years ago. Every time I called her she would tell me stories of other people's problems. My aunt did something strange. My uncle did something even stranger. Someone who is a distant relative ended up in an embarrassing situation. Someone in my father's business stole money from him.

She had a habit of telling me about people and their problems. After every conversation with her, I felt tired. I wanted to be excited to talk to her, but instead, I dreaded our conversations *(I was honest with mom about this eventually and she doesn't do this anymore—thank goodness)*.

Unfortunately, this is something that often happens in the workplace.

I'm talking about that team member who never stops complaining about everything that is wrong with the world. How about the person who's always in some kind of trouble? There's an endless string of "situations" or challenges or problems to solve.

I have a low threshold for problems. I don't see problems, only opportunities. When someone comes to me with a problem—aside from what's happening for them emotionally, which could range from needing attention to being in despair—it's an opportunity for me to create a solid relationship with this person.

I do this by using a simple model to get to the truth about people and their problems.

The most important thing to do is understand the type of "problems" people want you to solve for them and I believe there are only three main categories:

1. Problems that are really a cry for attention
2. Problems that create an authentic connection
3. Problems that are actually challenges

Let's look at the first category—the cry for attention. This is the most common type of problem. The type that you are most likely to encounter. Drama in the office. Gossip. Someone said something and someone got hurt. This person doesn't get on with that person. This type of problem is the easiest to solve. If your tolerance level for this type of problem is low, all you have to do is nothing—refrain from responding. Over time, you'll notice that nobody brings this type of problem to you anymore. My team does not come to me for attention. They know I have no time for that and they get no response from me.

Now, for the second category—problems that create an authentic connection.

There is a real human need for your Home Team to connect with you and they may talk to you about a problem that is happening in their lives because they trust you and value your advice. This problem could be around something they've overcome or it could be an ongoing challenge they're experiencing in their personal lives. Pay close attention when you have this type of problem in front of you. These are problems that matter because they're important to the people who are important to you. Make every effort to help as much as you can when your Home Team shares a problem like this.

Finally, the third category—problems that are actually challenges.

This is when your team needs you to put your "smart hat" on. They may be dealing with something they think is extremely harmful or even devastating to the business. They might freeze or feel fearful. When this happens, you need to come up with a solution so things can get back to normal.

The thing to remember is that most of the people on your team don't want to run their own business. They don't want the challenges and uncertainty that come with being an entrepreneur. They are happy to join you and focus on your direction and purpose. They enjoy the security of having a job and they enjoy the satisfaction of a job well done.

This also means your employees have a much lower tolerance for insecurity than you do.

They have a lower tolerance for doing the hard things.

They have a lower tolerance for understanding and identifying a serious problem as opposed to a challenge.

This is why you must correctly categorize the "problem"—otherwise, you're likely to end up running around putting out fires that aren't really fires.

Once you've mastered the art of categorizing problems, it's time to focus on the "people" part of the equation. People are complex, emotional beings. The greatest minds in the world have been trying for centuries to make sense of what makes human beings tick. We have tried to understand by studying biology, chemistry, psychology, and spirituality.

Despite all of this effort, human beings remain a mystery. There is still so much we don't know about ourselves—the mind and the body—even with all of our amazing technological advances. Do you know they found a new muscle in the human leg just about a year ago? They still don't know why we all have DMT receptors in the human body but no apparent use for DMT for our well-being and health.

There is so much we don't know, but there is also a lot that we *do* know.

Celebrated Swiss psychologist Carl Jung, one of the greatest minds in the field, presented a fascinating theory about human behavior: we act the way we do as a function of two primary factors—our experiences in the past and our aspirations for the future.

Once we understand what our past is and what our aspirations for the future are, we can pretty much project or predict how any individual will behave in any situation. Combine this revelation with Abraham Maslow's theory on motivation and you have a clear blueprint that will help you understand people.

Maslow's 1943 paper, "A Theory of Human Motivation," suggests that we follow a hierarchy of needs. You probably remember some of this from high school. First, we fulfill our basic human needs, like food, shelter, and safety. Then we look at how we can satisfy our need for belonging, friendship, love, and connection. As those needs are fulfilled, we then start to look at what we can do to fuel our self-esteem, which is essentially our need to feel that we matter and that our lives have purpose. Finally, we have the need for self-actualization. This is our need to feel like we are hitting our highest potential. This is often also understood as the need for growth and contribution.

Our past defines how we understand these needs. What does love mean for us? What does connection mean for us? How does it differ based on our experiences in life? Circumstances and events that happen in each of our lives create a different understanding of each of these needs.

If we can understand the internal stories of the people around us and our team members—their experiences of their own past and their aspirations for their future—we will instantly see what those different needs mean for each of them, as individuals. What makes them feel loved? What makes them feel safe? What makes them feel they have a purpose in life and that their lives have meaning?

As we develop these insights about people, we gain a deep understanding about how they view problems. This powerful knowledge will help us navigate through every problem that comes at us in business and turn each one into an opportunity. **An opportunity to grow and to learn and to overcome.**

To dive deeper into this topic, download free tools and advanced strategies at www.LiveBigTheBook.com/Tools.

TIME CHAL-LENGE

CHAPTER 21

The Time Challenge

*Let your life lightly dance on the edges of Time
like dew on the tip of a leaf.*

—Rabindranath Tagore

Stephen King has written so many bestsellers that it's hard to keep count. He is undoubtedly one of the most successful and brilliant fiction authors of modern times. In his book about writing, simply called *On Writing*, King describes his work schedule. Now, keep in mind that this is a highly creative person. Most of us have a preconceived idea about creative people resisting "the rules." We believe they hate structure and schedules and that they're all about "going with the flow." When we're dealing with a creative genius, we're even okay with them acting kind of crazy.

But there's no trace of craziness in King's routine. King reveals that he dedicates every morning to his newest book or whatever he happens to be writing at the moment. Afternoons are for naps and reading. Evenings are for family, games, and play.

Structured. Simple. Most important—effective.

One of the most important concepts I've learned about
structured scheduling and time can be found in a book called
The One Thing. This phenomenal book by Gary Keller will give
you a deep understanding on the time conundrum and how
you can become a time management ninja. In the book, Keller
shares two key categories of time: clock time and event time.

Most of the world operates on clock time and if you've ever
worked in an office, you're very familiar with this. The clock
hits 9 AM. Start work. Clock shows 5 PM. Stop work. This is
perfect if you happen to be doing simple, monotonous tasks on
a factory line. You probably feel very little—or zero—passion
for your work. You're expected to repeat the same activity again
and again. You quickly get to a point when you can do this with
your eyes shut and one hand tied behind your back. It's boring
beyond belief. This is an effort-based environment, which is
why clock time works so well.

Let's move on to event-based time. This is all about the end
game. Event time is about dedicating yourself to a task until
you reach the expected outcome. There's been no outcome
yet? Keep going until you get there. This is the kind of time
we work with as entrepreneurs and it also applies to anyone
whose work requires deep thinking and intellectual reasoning
and creativity—knowledge work.

For the longest time, I had no idea that event time existed.
In India, where I grew up, it's all about the 9 to 5 schedule. It's
all about when you come into the office. It's about going home
only after your boss has left the building. Everyone followed
this structure without question. It seemed to be the most effective and efficient way to do things.

This process and belief system was deeply ingrained in my mind. I absolutely had to see every one of my team members at their desk at 9 AM sharp each morning, typing like the wind at their computers or at least looking like they were doing something useful. And I expected them to stay there until 5 PM—preferably longer. If I didn't see someone at the office during those hours, it was a problem for me. A major problem. I'd start getting antsy and anxious. I'd start asking all kinds of questions.

What do you mean you're working from home?

Why did you take so long to get back from lunch?

Where were you after that meeting? I didn't see you at your desk!

This went on until I started to notice that the actual work that we accomplished did not match the number of hours we put into doing things. I decided to get real. I paid attention to my own behavior at the office and I discovered something I didn't like. I realized that even if I was physically sitting in the office throughout the day—and half the night—I achieved very little during that time. If I'm being perfectly honest, a lot of my time in the office was spent doing nothing.

I had a million distractions, which meant I only managed to put in a few hours of solid work in a day. Most days, I was sitting at my desk for about ten hours and accomplishing less than four hours of work. I was working hard, yes, but I wasn't being effective.

I observed the same behavior in my best performers. When they were in flow, when they were in the zone, all they needed was three to four hours to complete a full day of productive work. But that wasn't the only amazing thing I noticed. I realized that the *quality* of their work seemed to have an odd relationship with the amount of time they spent on it.

Interestingly enough, the quality of their work didn't necessarily increase the more time they spent getting it done. Turns out, there is no real connection between the amount of time you spend doing something and the quality you manage to deliver. Quality is a factor of your *internal state* and not the amount of time you spend. If you are in a state of flow, the quality of what you do rises dramatically.

What's going on here is a combination of the Flow State, which we explored in chapter 7, and Parkinson's Law. We are in a state of flow when we have something exciting or challenging to work on and when we know we have the skills to get it done right. Meanwhile, Parkinson's Law states: work expands so as to fill the time available for its completion.

This means that when we give ourselves a specific time block to complete each of our tasks, we can actually "artificially" induce flow. By adding time as a challenge to the situation, we are, in fact, forcing our brain to access a state that would otherwise be difficult—or even impossible—to reach. This leads to exciting possibilities for entrepreneurs.

Twenty-first-century businesses are almost exclusively reliant on the efficiency of their knowledge workers. Now that so many of these businesses are online, there is a high likelihood that you will work with people from around the world. Virtual assistants, copywriters you've never met, project managers who live in a different time zone. Even in the "traditional" office space, there is a significant, notable increase in the "work from home" culture.

So, let me ask you this enticing question—what if we could let go of clock time altogether? What if we forget about 9 to 5? What if we all decide to focus on the outcome we want to achieve? What if we start hiring for the results produced and not time spent? What if we induced flow to achieve incredible results?

When I adopted this viewpoint, it transformed my relationship with my employees—especially those who worked remotely. I stopped looking at their time logs because I realized that it didn't matter. The only elements that matter are effectiveness and results. As long as my team gets their tasks done on time or ahead of our schedule, I'm a happy camper.

This shift in thinking didn't just change the relationship I had with my team—it changed the relationship I had with myself. I'm no longer hard on myself in the way I used to be. When I get things done for the day, I don't feel guilty about leaving early. I don't feel bad about enjoying a longer lunch in the middle of the day or getting a relaxing massage in the middle of the week.

My time is no longer governed by the clock. I'm no longer a slave to it. Now it's all about the outcome for me. Our greatest asset, our greatest resource, is time. Time is life and time cannot be replenished. When it's gone, you don't get it back. Now that I operate on event based time, I'm finally maximizing my greatest asset—my time.

My life is about what I want to achieve. The end result. Not a random number on the face of a clock.

To dive deeper into this topic, download free tools and advanced strategies at www.LiveBigTheBook.com/Tools.

DISCIPLINE PROGRESS

 DELEGATE

 AUTOMATE

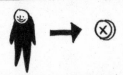 DELETE

CHAPTER 22

The Discipline of Progress

Discipline is the bridge between goals and accomplishment.

—Jim Rohn

There's a coaching company I know that went from an annual revenue of six figures to $2.5 million in just over twelve months. This triggered two things: the owners set even more outrageous goals for themselves the following year and everyone in the company began to feel the heat. They were overwhelmed and the team was under a lot pressure to produce results.

One of my clients recently experienced a similar situation. They had created a product that worked like magic. They had the right marketing channels and tools that could communicate that magic to their customers. They had a rockstar team that could help to deliver the magic. It was like sunrise over the hills of Malibu.

Perfect. Except that it wasn't.

They were growing faster than they could handle and it was all beginning to get to them. They were working way too many hours. The work that had felt so inspiring and creative was no longer interesting. The team was stretched to the limit. Everyone was constantly tired and frustrated.

When we make progress—especially, if we make stratospheric, exponential progress—we need to fall back on a principle that pretty much every entrepreneur in the world hates with a passion: discipline. Discipline is something we resist, it's something we want to escape. It's something we don't ever want to think about.

If you've tried bulletproof coffee, you know that the first sip you ever take is pretty disgusting. For those of you who have no idea what I'm talking about here, bulletproof coffee is essentially coffee with a bit of fat in it. As you can imagine, this is going to taste weird. The first time you drink it, you want to wash your mouth out with soap—I'm not even kidding! But as you keep drinking, as you stay open to the experience and think of the benefits of having fat in your coffee *(and there's a whole bunch of benefits—just look it up)*, you'll start to like it. Over time, you might even fall in love with it.

Practicing discipline is exactly the same. It's a pain in the ass when you first try it, but over time, it brings you unimaginable benefits and significant progress. I personally think learning how to stay disciplined is the greatest gift you can ever give yourself.

Now, back to that overwhelmed client I mentioned:

They got to the breaking point. It was complete chaos in that company. The owners came to me, desperate to make changes. I told them this: "From here on out, I want you to look at every task, every activity inside your company, and ask yourself: 'How can I never do this task again?'"

How can I never do this task again?

Start with this simple, powerful question and you'll be naturally drawn to answer the three other related questions. *Why* am I doing this task? Do I *really need* to do this task?

And then you arrive at the winning question:

How can I delegate, automate, or delete this task?

Delegate.

Automate.

Delete.

Most of the tasks that we carry out, most of the work that we feel most passionate about when we are starting a business, become the very things that get in our way as the business grows. I was passionate about figuring out the technology that powered our websites when I first started my business, and the same went for design. I wanted to go into every little detail. I spent hours looking at each page, thinking about how I could make it look better. I loved every part of it.

But this passion—okay, obsession—created a lot of stress for my team. They were totally pissed off, especially the ones who were design experts, and I can't say I blame them. They were the ones who had spent a lot of time coming up with the design, coming up with the code, making sure it all functioned perfectly. And I would come in with my ideas and interfere.

I learned soon enough that this is undisciplined behavior and if you want to be a successful entrepreneur you need to get over it fast. You don't need to know how everything works. You don't need to be an expert at *everything*. You just need to be an expert at one thing—bringing all of the pieces together so they work in harmony.

Think of your business as an orchestra and you as the conductor. Let the drummer do his thing on the drums. Allow the violinist to create magic with the violin. Your job—the discipline that you must practice—is to focus on leading the entire orchestra to create beautiful music. An entrepreneur who goes into every little detail in his or her business is like a music conductor trying to play every instrument in the orchestra at the same time. There is no discipline in this and it's not going to work.

Delegate to experts. Delegate to skilled people who are ready to spend time on the details—far more time than you ever could or should.

And when you can't delegate, automate.

Automate through software, AI, or machinery. Take your pick. I was once hired as a business consultant for a neurofeedback company. They have several clinics and they work on advanced methods of neurofeedback. They were great at what they did, but so many potential customers never had the chance to find this out for themselves. The reason? It was a huge challenge just to book an appointment with them.

Here's what you had to do:

Step 1. Go to their website and find their number.

Step 2. Call that number.

Step 3. Leave a voice message and share your phone number.

Step 4. They would then call you back to schedule an appointment.

The result of this complex, convoluted, and crazy appointment booking system is that 60 percent of the potential customers who left a voice message never answered their phone when the company called them back to schedule an appointment. At best, it took several weeks to have customers schedule an appointment because the team had to call the customer again and again before they finally answered the phone.

The first thing I did when I stepped in was to implement automation. Here's what their booking process looked like after I was done:

Step 1. Go to their website and click on a button to book an appointment.

Step 2. Schedule an appointment on the digital calendar that pops up.

That was it.

After automation, 100 percent of the potential customers who wanted to book an appointment could do so immediately. No missed phone calls. No delays. Automating the booking process with the addition of a simple calendar form on their website was all that was needed to increase results by a full 100 percent. You can now look at automating extraordinarily complex tasks with technology. If that feels a little outside your comfort zone, then look at how you can start automating some of the simpler tasks first.

We've covered delegate and automate. Now we're up against the most challenging of the three—delete. You've probably heard of Pareto's Principle, which is also popularly known as the 80/20 rule. According to this principle, you get about 80 percent of your results with 20 percent of effort. If we look at our workflow, our business ecosystem, we will come to see that we only have to do 20 percent of the work to get most of our sales and profits.

This is powerful information, but here's what I have found to be even more powerful. Take the 80/20 rule and hone in on the 20 percent that gives you 80 percent of the results you're looking for. Now, write down the remaining 80 percent of tasks that gets you just 20 percent of the results. Out of this second category of tasks, if you drop 50 percent and keep 50 percent, you'll end up with 95 percent of the results you want for your business.

If you have no idea what I mean, let me illustrate with an example.

Let's say there are a hundred tasks that need to be done in your business. When you apply Pareto's Principle, you'll find that twenty tasks create 80 percent of the results and eighty tasks create 20 percent of the results. Out of those eighty tasks that create 20 percent of the results, there are forty tasks that will give you an additional 15 percent of the results. When you add both, you'll end up with sixty out of the hundred tasks that create 95 percent of the results you want in your business. This also means you can delete the remaining forty tasks and create new opportunities for yourself. More important, you can create more time for yourself and your team.

Delegate. Automate. Delete. It's the only way to go. It's the only way to grow.

To dive deeper into this topic, download free tools and advanced strategies at www.LiveBigTheBook.com/Tools.

VALUE

VALUE

VALUE

CHAPTER 23

Value. Value. Value. Value. Value.

Try not to become a man of success, but rather try to become a man of value.

—Albert Einstein

Juan is a brilliant man with a thick Latin American accent. I met him during his stratospheric rise at Mindvalley. I remember the day when Juan rocked me to my core. It's one of those moments in life—a single moment—that changes everything.

We were walking to a favorite lunch spot in the heart of Kuala Lumpur on an extra hot, humid day. We had to raise our voices so we could hear each other above the raucous sounds of the city streets. It was easy to get distracted, but Juan had my undivided attention.

He was telling me the story of how he was hired.

I'd heard through the grapevine that Juan had joined Mindvalley under some pretty unusual circumstances, but I wasn't sure of the details. I knew it was going to be one heck of a story and I was eager to hear it from the man himself. It would give me insight into his thinking. I was all set to hear the entire tale and I expected him to include flourishes and drama—all the details storytellers love to share. But Juan isn't one to waste time, even when he's telling a great story. He summed up the entire account in a single sentence.

"At my interview, I gave Mindvalley a personal guarantee. If I didn't get them the results they were looking for, I would return every cent they paid me."

This revelation stopped me in my tracks. Who in their right mind gives a guarantee at a job interview? When a company hires, the risk is on them and not on the candidate interviewing for the job. A personal guarantee at a job interview? I'd never heard of such a thing. Most of us think, *If I get a job, I'm going to be busting my ass for the company! Why would I give them a guarantee and risk losing my salary?* Most of us think a job interview is about what we can get, not what we can give.

But Juan isn't "most of us." He continued, "Back in Argentina, I sold everything from charcoal pieces to ships. I knew what I was doing then. I knew exactly what was in it for me. I knew what I could do and what I couldn't do. But with Mindvalley, I was entering a whole new world. I knew I had to do something no one else was willing to do or would even dream of doing to get that job. They were looking for value and I was willing to go all out to give them that. That's why I gave that personal guarantee . . . and I meant every word."

On the day I heard this story, when we were walking down that humid, noisy street in Malaysia, Juan was headed straight for the COO's seat at Mindvalley—a world class, transformational learning company. He eventually did sit in the COO's chair, but he didn't stop there.

Juan went on to become an incredibly successful private investor. He now owns businesses that generate millions in sales across Latin America. He lives with his family in Argentina and is recognized and honored as one of only a handful of marketing geniuses in his country.

Most of us imagine that if we provide value in our work, we should get paid—we *must* get paid. This is a valid argument. But it's useless when it comes to business. Yes, I know it's not a fair trade, but you need to get over it.

The real deal is that you must give value for free. And then do it again and again and again.

You can give value by sharing transformational information. You can choose to give away your product or part of your service. You can give value by getting on a free call with a potential client and giving them a real solution to a current problem or challenge. Or, like Juan, you can offer free value by giving a bold, out-of-the-ordinary, hit-me-between-the-eyes guarantee. People think they can give away too much value. But this is a myth because there is no such thing as too much value.

I want you to reflect on your life.

How many times did you have to go through the same challenge or some version of the same difficult experience before you learned what you needed to learn? For instance, how many of us end up dating the same kind of person, who just isn't right for us, before we finally free ourselves from the vicious cycle?

We end up with serial cheaters. Again and again. We end up with the "bad" boy or girl. The person who doesn't return our calls. The one who ignores our needs. This can go on for months or years before we finally realize we deserve better.

Intellectually, we understand we're attracted to the wrong person. We know we should date someone who truly cares, but it takes multiple conversations with friends, a therapist, or a coach, hours of watching old episodes of the *Oprah Winfrey Show*, or reading books like *The Secret to a Successful Romance* and *How to Find Mr./Ms. Right (okay, I'm making up these titles, but you get the picture)*.

This is life. This is the human experience. Often, we need to learn the same lesson again and again before we finally get it. For good. The same theory applies in business. Your clients and customers go through the same challenges or problems again and again and you can provide your solutions again and again. Every time you expand your tribe or your audience and more potential customers and clients enter your space, you have even more people with similar challenges and problems who need you and your solutions.

There is no such thing as too much free value. As human beings, we need the same conversation again and again before we can rise above our struggles and challenges. You don't have to reinvent the wheel here. You can keep creating and sharing free value from the same content, product, or service until the end of time, and it will never get old.

Still sound a little too simplistic and hard to believe?

Maybe you're thinking, "So Ajit, what you're saying here is the more value and solutions I give away for free, the more successful I become?" Yes, that's exactly what I'm saying. I call it the Super Correlation: the more value you create for free, the more prosperous, profitable, and successful you will become.

Don't take my word for it. Look around and you'll see the Super Correlation at work, all around.

Take Tony Robbins.

He's known around the world as a master coach and speaker. Robbins rose from nothing all the way to the extraordinarily successful entrepreneur, author, philanthropist, and coach he is today. And he did it by sharing the same advice from day one.

The next time you're in a bookstore *(or if it's on your shelf, go get it now),* take a look at one of his first books, *Awaken the Giant Within,* which he wrote back in 1991. It's about taking control of your life and your future. It's a great book. Now, skim through the contents page. Next, search for any one of Robbins's latest, free online talks on YouTube and watch a couple of minutes of it. You'll start to see he's talking about pretty much the same concepts that you can find in *Awaken the Giant Within.* He's been doing this for years. Decades.

Now, here's the truly "shocking" bit. Everyone loves hearing his insights and advice. Again and again. People are even willing to pay to hear the same advice. I've heard of people who've attended his live events every year, since the early nineties.

This isn't crazy. It's a fact of life. And it's a fact in business.

Give away value for free again and again and people will pay to hear what you have to say and learn what you have to teach. People will purchase your services, books, seminar tickets, programs, and products.

Even better—they'll be happy to do it.

The same concept was at play when we built Mindvalley from the ground up. It's an incredibly successful company today, but we didn't get here by charging crazy, high prices for everything.

We got here by charging nothing. To this day, we give away 95 percent of our trainings, absolutely free. No charges whatsoever. What's for sale is just 5 percent of what we have.

Five percent. That's it.

Mindvalley is a multimillion dollar company and it's still growing. This is the Super Correlation at work. It's about creating incredible, free value out in the world. It's why we have so many fans who love what we do and who are ready to purchase from us.

The payoff is tremendous.

We've found that so many of our high-end clients started out by implementing our free information, ideas, and teachings. Then, they go on to build successful businesses and come back to us two or three years later to purchase our top-level programs and the counseling of our masterminds. These clients are happy to pay thousands of dollars to continue that relationship and work with us for one simple reason—and this leads me straight to the next insight—the Guarantee.

Why does the Super Correlation work so well? Because it creates the most important element in business (and in life): trust.

If you give away value without expecting anything in return, and you're continuously doing this and creating results for your clients, you will reap the rewards over time. Guaranteed. These rewards include loyal, lifelong fans, recognition of your expertise and genius, maybe even worldwide fame, and, yes, money. A lot of it.

So, it goes like this:

Value, value, value, value, value → *Trust*

And with trust comes an amazing depth of emotion that creates an unbreakable bond.

It's a connection that will make your customers smile when they think of your company and your services. It's a feeling of knowing they're in good hands when they come to you for solutions. This is how you create an ultra-successful business that matters. A business that continues to grow and expand. A business that continues to bring in more and more income.

It all starts with giving value away for free. And it works. Every time.

To dive deeper into this topic, download free tools and advanced strategies at www.LiveBigTheBook.com/Tools.

DIFFE-
RENT

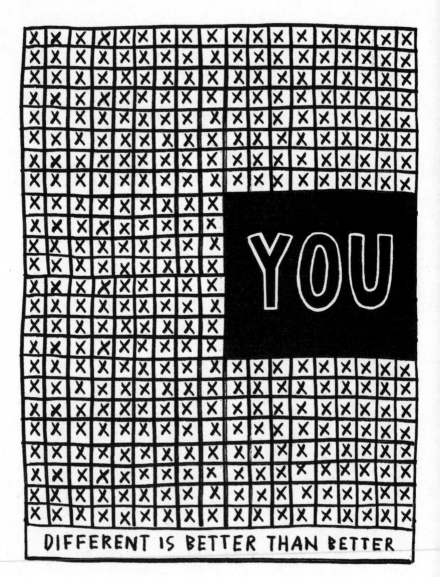

DIFFERENT IS BETTER THAN BETTER

CHAPTER 24

Different

In order to be irreplaceable one must always be different.

—Coco Chanel

Every once in a while, a book turns up in our collective consciousness and it changes the way we see the world. W. Chan Kim and Renee Mauborgne's *Blue Ocean Strategy: How to Create Uncontested Market Space and Make Competition Irrelevant* did exactly this in 2005.

It's a revolutionary book that turned the concept of competition in business on its head.

The book was a result of Kim and Mauborgne's research on the world's most successful companies over the past hundred years. It was soon clear that the secret behind these companies' success and their longevity—despite turbulent markets, economic downturns, and catastrophic world events—could be compressed into just one thing: they created "a blue ocean" or an uncontested market in their industry.

They aren't the best player on the board. They are the *only* player.

Most businesses are drowning in a sea of endless competition. All of their energy, focus, and resources go into creating a product or service that's better than the next guy's. Sometimes they don't even manage to do that. They just produce the same thing at a lower price. This is not the way great companies do business. The world's most successful companies may appear to operate in the same competitive space as everyone else, but when you look closely, you'll see they are very different.

Let's look at Tesla.

Tesla makes cars, mainly sedans and SUVs. They're an automotive company. It even says so on their website. But when you go deeper, you'll see Tesla is not like any other automotive company on the planet. For one thing, Tesla owns its distribution channel. It creates premium products exclusively. It manufactures only electric cars. Tesla speaks to the affluent customer who cares about the world. The customer who loves efficiency. The customer who loves technology. This is why Tesla swims in a Blue Ocean. The company dominates the "electric car" category. Even if you happen to drive an electric car that is not a Tesla, your car probably operates on batteries manufactured by the company.

Tesla is in the same automotive industry as their competitors but they're not the same.

Tesla is different.

And different is better.

Different is *better* than better.

When you are different, you have an opportunity to work in a new marketplace and with clients who are desperately looking for solutions. When this happens, you get to make the rules because you're pretty much the only one who can provide those solutions. You get to create a vision and a mission for an entire category.

This is also how Apple did it. Back in 2003, Apple's iTunes store and music downloading were the epitome of innovation. Before iTunes, you were forced to purchase clunky CDs if you wanted to own the music you love. Your only other option was illegal downloads. Apple changed all that. The company transformed the way people bought and listened to music.

Apple is in the same music distribution industry as their competitors, but they're not the same.

Apple is different.

And different is better.

Different is *better* than better.

You might have heard of Evercoach. It's a learning portal for coaches around the world who are looking to elevate their game. You can find thousands of other portals—programs, teachers, organizations—dedicated to helping coaches. They'll show you how to be a better coach and how to build a business around coaching. None of them bring the teachings of top coaches in the industry to coaches around the world quite like we do.

Evercoach is in the same teaching and coaching space as our competitors, but we're not the same.

Evercoach is different.

And different is better.

Different is *better* than better.

You might have looked at a market leader in your niche and wondered, "How can I create the same kind of success?" This isn't the right question to ask yourself. If you want to create the same kind of success, you have to step into the same playing field as that market leader. You will have to compete. When you compete to be better than someone else, there's a simple truth you might not want to accept but it's a truth you must face.

The person or the company you're competing against is *already better than you*. This is the only reason you're inspired to hit their level of success because they have more success than you do.

If they're leaders in the industry, they'll never stop growing. They're probably working as hard as you—maybe even harder. So, if you want to beat them at this game, you have your work cut out for you. And let me tell you now, you're probably not going to win.

To compete is to chase and never catch up.

To be different is to create your own space.

And to create your own space is to *own* that space.

Be different. Different is always better. It's *better* than better.

To dive deeper into this topic, download free tools and advanced strategies at www.LiveBigTheBook.com/Tools.

MAKE
MONEY

CHAPTER 25

$

Life started getting good when I started making money.

—Balthazar Getty

Build it and they will come. This was the mantra of Silicon Valley. The startup community. The mantra we entrepreneurs are asked to live by.

Following that mantra, I started a technology company years ago. It was unique in India at that time. This was a well-funded startup that focused on social networks. At the time, Facebook had yet to reach India. We thought if we made something fun, something interesting, something that was a truly great product, "they" would come.

We built it. Rebuilt it. Corrected it. Tweaked it.

Surprisingly—or, come to think of it, maybe not so surprisingly—no one came.

Well, some people did turn up, but definitely not enough.

Not enough to make the platform viable.

Not enough to keep going.

Now, you might think, *Maybe what you built was kind of shitty and that's why they didn't come.* I won't argue. I could have done much better. We can always do better. But let me tell you what we created wasn't that bad. The technology was ahead of its time. The interface was clean and easy. It was fun to use.

And we were genuinely surprised when no one cared.

This initial failure didn't stop me. I built many things after that first product and I helped build even more things with others that were and are amazing. But no one came and no one ever will. Not until we do all of the things we need to do to invite, entice, and attract people.

It's called customer service. It's called sales. It's called marketing.

Build it and they will come is one of the biggest lies about entrepreneurship out there. It kills more dreams than any other lie. It's like a knife straight through the heart.

Build it.

Then do what it takes to invite them to try. To taste. To experience. To fall in love with your product or service. When you start making money, put it right back in the business and do it all over again. And again. And again.

This is the truth of how it works. We know it instinctively, but somehow we all want to believe in the romance of *build it and they will come.*

My wife, Neeta, runs a retreat for writers twice a year. One of the exercises she has everyone go through is called the Collective. The Collective is about using the power of the group to brainstorm an idea. This allows a lot of space for creativity.

I attended one of Neeta's retreats and during the Collective exercise, one of the writers—she's an entrepreneur who's been in the game for twenty years—shared details of how she planned to connect her book back to her business. She talked about how the book would translate to more revenue. The entrepreneur knew the book would go places. She knew she had an audience who'd be happy to read her book.

Another writer in the group was disappointed when he heard this plan. He couldn't understand how the first writer had laid out her entire business plan but hadn't shared the heartfelt story of *why* she wanted to write the book in the first place. He felt the first writer was focused on finances and revenue. It was about the money. Not about the heart, soul, and pleasure of writing a book.

Here's what I want to tell you and it's something that may surprise or even shock you:

Money is important. It is crucial. It is the lifeblood of your business. It doesn't matter whether you want to change the world or you just want to change your own life—whatever your intention, you must make money first. There are many well-intentioned messages out there to motivate entrepreneurs. Find your "why," follow your destiny, discover your purpose, do it to change the world.

All great advice but also absolutely useless until and unless you start making money.

If you don't, it's all over.

There are great stories about Facebook or Google or even Apple doing it all to serve and to change the world. This is cute. It's adorable. I love these stories. But don't let these touching tales cloud the truth.

These are incredibly successful companies with mind-blowing profits. They didn't do it all just by following their heart. At some point, they sat down and figured out how to pitch to investors. They figured out how to get funding. They figured out how to grow and expand without going into the red.

They figured out how to make money and so should you.

Create an amazing product. Put your blood, sweat, and tears into it. But put in the same effort to create sales. I'm going to be brutally honest and say that you should put in *more* effort to create sales. Especially when you are just starting out.

I learned this lesson the hard way when my first venture in India turned to dust. We didn't make the same mistake twice. With the second company, the focus was on money first. We were talking about and planning on how to make money long before we had a finished product in place. We sold that company to a much larger corporation in just a few months.

And because we knew how we would make money, it was an easy sale.

Money matters in business. Always has. Always will. Live that truth and you'll see there's no limit to how high you'll fly.

To dive deeper into this topic, download free tools and advanced strategies at www.LiveBigTheBook.com/Tools.

AN ARGUMENT
FOR LOVE

Somewhere along the way . . .

As we work hard to build a successful business . . .

As we study hard at a prestigious business school . . .

As we become lost in that overwhelming drive to create something magical . . .

As we try to fill the emptiness in our hearts with work . . .

We forget *why* we're doing it all.

Why do we create, innovate, and build? Why do we put ourselves out there? What is that burning need inside us that drives us to sacrifice everything? What is it that pushes us to build our business with so much focus and persistence that we forget ourselves, our health, our well-being? That we end up sabotaging our cherished relationships? That we end up missing our child's first day at school? That we willingly give up time with loved ones?

We're doing it all—we're building, creating, growing a business—for love. When I say love, I don't mean romantic, steamy, sexual love.

I mean pure love.

Love that you might have for a spectacular piece of artwork. Love that you might have for travel and for new adventures. Love that you might have for the quiet beauty of snowfall.

This is the love that creates. The love that inspires. The love that we're doing it all for.

It's fascinating to see what happens when you introduce love to your business. Your creation.

When you let love in, your team seems to fall in love with what they do.

When you let love in, your clients show up for you. Defend you. Protect you. Cheer you on.

When you let love in, you have endless courage. Creativity. Clarity. Drive.

Love is behind it all. Love brings out the best in you. It brings out the best in your people. Love brings out the best in your business.

Apple decided to love their clients above all else. They would have store managers, not just assistants, call customers who needed help and spend as much time as necessary on the phone "to make things right." This is an expensive thing to do. But Apple found that each hour their managers spent on the phone, an additional one thousand dollars in sales would be generated.

Loving your customers isn't just a good idea. It's smart business.

When we introduced what we call "sugar cubes"— anonymously sharing love notes with participants during live Evercoach events—people shared a lot more about our event on social media and many of them attended our next event and our next.

When we introduced "love week" in our company, we not only became a case study for other companies, it skyrocketed satisfaction within our teams. We've found that making friends with your coworkers didn't just inspire amazing team members to continue working with us, it increased the quality of their work.

Love works. Loving each other works. Loving your team works. Loving your clients works.

I know that sometimes, it feels like the bad guys win. I know it feels like the world tells you that you need to be a hard-nosed, slimy, asshole entrepreneur to get to the top. But that's not true. Sooner or later the bad guys lose.

In the end, love always wins. Always.

So, remember your why. Why do you want to win? What do you want to win? What is it that really matters to you?

You might have heard of this old saying: *It's not personal, it's business.*

Wrong.

Business is personal. It always has been. There is no other way we could keep doing what we do. There is no other reason to wake up every day and run your business.

Let love in. Fuel everything with all the love you have.

Then watch your business take off. Watch your vision and your goals come to life when your team and your clients support you with love.

Business is love.

Know this. Understand this. Embody this.

Live by this.

It's how you stay true to yourself.

It's how you make the impossible possible.

It's how you experience authentic success and happiness.

It's how you Live Big.

ACKNOWLEDGMENTS

This book was nothing more than a dream for me for the longest time. I am deeply fortunate to have all the right dream makers show up to make this book a reality.

To my beautiful, powerful magic maker, Neeta. You are the love of my life and my rock. Thank you for your support and your brilliance throughout the writing of this book. Thank you for always being there for me. Thank you for being you.

To Vishen Lakhiani, for believing in me when I was that unsure twenty-something who didn't know the first thing about building a meaningful business and creating changes that matter. You have shown me that we can achieve anything and everything we set our hearts and minds to. You have been my trusted mentor, my true friend, and an incredible inspirational force in my life. Thank you for all that you are and all that you do.

To the team at Evercoach by Mindvalley: Alina, Siddharth, Ana, Brian, Mattew, Toma, and Francesca. Without you I wouldn't have the strength to show up as powerfully as I do. Without you I wouldn't have the creative insights to reach and help so many people around the world. Without you, I wouldn't be who I am and where I am today. Thank you for being the stars in my life that light the way.

To Shantini, my collaborator. Thank you for beautifully capturing the essence of this book, and for making my writing shine. Thank you for helping me bring through the message in my heart that I want to share with the world.

A special shout out to everyone at Epic Businesses, especially Himanshu, for being the maestro that you are and flawlessly bringing all of the tech pieces together so they make music.

To my beloved family: my parents, Ashok and Chandrakala; my brother and sister-in-law, Atul and Siddhi; and my nephews, Avish and Aarush. To my in-laws Bua and Uncle Glenn and Neeta's brother, Vinay. You keep us going every day. You are our inspiration, our life's mission, and the reason we do what we do. Every one of you will live in my heart forever.

And last, but not least, to you—the extraordinary, soulful entrepreneur.

Thank you for choosing this book.

Thank you for looking for the answers.

Thank you for being who you are.

Thank you for wanting to change the world.

Because you can and you will.

Serve, first.

Love, always.

—Ajit

ABOUT THE AUTHOR

© Paulius Staniunas

A̲jit Nawalkha, a serial entrepreneur, global educator, and consultant, is the co-founder of Mindvalley Teach, Ever-coach, and Global GRIT Institute. Born in Jaipur, Rajasthan, where he grew up in a home with twenty-three other people, Ajit has always pursued the dream of Living Big. Over the past decade he has helped build training and coaching companies to inspire the coming generation, transforming entrepreneurs to live with purpose and enjoy their lives while increasing profits. He enjoys exploring the world, learning different cuisines, writing, and spending time with his wife, Neeta. He currently lives in Los Angeles, California.

Ajit loves connecting and discussing ideas of growth with his readers. Connect with Ajit on these social media platforms:

Instagram: instagram.com/ajitnawalkha
Linkedin: linkedin.com/in/ajitnawalkha/
Facebook: facebook.com/ajit.nawalkha
You can also email Ajit at: livebig@ajitnawalkha.com